# COME QUITTIN' TIME

## From Child Laborer to Family Matriarch, a Mother's Lifetime Spent in Southern Cotton Mills

OTHER BOOKS BY WILT BROWNING

Linthead

The Rocks

Deadly Goals

Saying Goodbye

# COME QUITTIN' TIME

## From Child Laborer to Family Matriarch, a Mother's Lifetime Spent in Southern Cotton Mills

# Wilt Browning
### with
### Marlene Burke and Doris Browning

Published by Alabaster Book Publishing
North Carolina

Published by Alabaster Book Publishing
P.O. Box 401
Kernersville, North Carolina 27285

Book design by
D.L.Shaffer
Cover design by Tammy Rogers

First Edition

ISBN:978-0-9790949-2-7

Library of Congress Control
Number: 2007903526

Dedicated To
The 11 Grandchildren

Ken
Vicky
Tim
Mark
Tammy
Jenny
Sherri
Deanna
Thomas
Andy
Bryan

# *Acknowledgments*

When my sisters and I were school-age children, we frequently disagreed about the division of chores in the Browning household. But there were no disagreements more vocal or more frequent than those having to do with dinner dishes, and it always came down to the question of which of us would wash, and which of us would do the drying. I never envisioned a career in either specialty, but drying, if it had to be done at all, was my stronger suit. The disagreements at the kitchen sink frequently had to be settled by one of our parents and Dad wound up posting an assignment sheet. I grumbled even about that because it meant that I would have to take my turn dipping my hands into the hot dish water and scrubbing away the residue of the meal just past.

---

**ABOUT THE COVER**

One of Martha and Willie Lee Browning's 11 grandchildren, Tammy Rogers, created the cover for Come Quittin' Time. She chose as the focal point a photo of her grandmother as a young beauty queen. A professional design artist, Tammy runs her own business, Roger's Design Studio, 125 Bracken Court, Liberty, SC, 29657.

I think, therefore, our parents would be pleased with the manner in which the three of us cheerfully joined hands in this work. I will now tell you something I would not have said in those years of washing dishes: I could not have done it without my sisters. The contributions of Marlene, whose memory for small detail is remarkable, and Doris, who opened her own life to aspects of her time as a child and then as a young lady on the mill hill, were absolutely essential. Personally, Doris went the extra mile, sharing with us deep, life-altering secrets even Mother and Dad apparently never knew.

I wish to thank, as well, a woman I barely know, Lorene Harrell, a former schoolteacher who once worked during summer school vacations in the mills at Kannapolis, North Carolina. She played a role more significant than she realized when she stopped by the table at the 2005 cotton mill convention where I was selling my first book, *Linthead*. There she offered me a well-organized file container jammed with mill hill information. She at one time had intended to write a book as well, she said, but now had decided against the project and left her research with me "just in case you are interested in maybe writing another book." Her gift helped jump-start this project, and I thank her for her generosity and encouragement.

My uncle, Clarence Browning, one of my Dad's brothers, was helpful in filling in some of the blanks, and his contributions are sincerely appreciated. Regrettably, this information came close to being lost. In the closing hours of February 2006 - no one is sure exactly when - Clarence apparently suffered a fatal heart attack. His wife and our aunt, Jett, bedridden for more than a decade, tried to reach her stricken husband and it is believed that she too suffered a life-ending coronary. They were interred side-by-side close to the resting places of our Mother and Father.

Jerry Bledsoe has been a close friend and fishing companion for a lot of years now, and he also is the editor and publisher of my first four books. In my opinion, he was perhaps the finest newspaper columnist I ever knew and a remarkably prolific and talented author. What most readers perhaps do not know about Jerry is that he is one of the two or three best editors who ever tried to make sense out of what I had written. I thank him for that and, most of all, for his unwavering support in so many ways over the years.

And I offer love and thanks to my wife, Joyce, who once again accepted without complaint my frequent retreats to my cave of an office where this book took its form, and for being my sounding board, as she always has been, in helping me understand the things I had learned, mostly about my mother.

In their own way, my children also lavished encouragement on me by asking without fail how the writing of the book based on the life of their grandmother was going. I thank them for caring.

They're gone now, but I also am eternally thankful that Mother and Dad were who they were, special parents in a special place at a special time.

Martha Chappell Browning:  June 1912 - December 2002

# *Prologue*

Folks at my mother's church used to tell me how proud she was of me. While still a teenager, I had gone away from the mill hill early, married young, spent my life writing for newspapers, mostly sports, had won a handful of journalism awards to stoke my ego, and had played a minor role in helping my wife raise our five children.

Though few become wealthy in the newspaper business, I may have earned in my lifetime more money than Mother and Dad together brought home for all of those years working in the cotton mills. Which is not to praise newspaper publishers as much as to make a statement about the standards of living in the shadow of cotton mills. I cannot be sure I earned more because we held such information as private, even within the family. I once had a school teacher who on one occasion gave her class the homework assignment of finding out and reporting the incomes of her students' fathers and mothers. The next day when my turn to report came, I told my teacher that the money my mother and father earned was certainly none of my business and, as far as I could tell, none of hers. Dad didn't even scold me when I told him why I had received a failing grade on that homework assignment.

I had made Mother proud in that flirtation with defiance, I was told. In that I was surprised, though I would learn later that I should not have been. There was a bit of a rebel in Mother that I had not known at the time.

As a high school student, I played the trumpet in the school band. I frequently practiced at home, squeezing almost as many bad notes from my King Super 20 as good ones. But Mother apparently heard only the good ones and, because the "music" was coming from the room I shared with my sisters, she felt that Gabriel himself must be listening.

My two sisters still contend, without outward signs of jealousy, that I was Mother's favorite.

I point all that wonderfulness out as a preamble to a confession here: I wish I had spent more of my life while she was with us appreciating my mother instead of basking in her appreciation of me.

She died at the age of 90 just before Christmas 2002. I missed her when she was gone and I know that I loved her. But in the months since her death I have discovered that she was far more remarkable than I had understood for most of my life. During her life, I knew she baked some of the best home-made biscuits anyone has ever tasted, that her coconut cakes were legendary, that like Dad she was faithful in the daily study of the Bible, but not only the Bible; her reading interests were almost as wide as the publishing field itself. Though her formal education ended almost as soon as it began, she taught herself how to read. And having done that, she could never get enough of the printed word. She read more books in her lifetime than many people have ever seen.

Those are among the things that I knew about the person who tucked me in when I was a child and who later welcomed my wife and our children to her table. I was less clear on other aspects of her life. Though as a newspaper man I should have known better, I regret that I never recorded her memories. What runs through this book are those I have but, more importantly, the memories and the stories relayed through my sisters, Marlene Burke and Doris Browning.

Because her life very closely paralleled that of the robust years of cotton manufacturing in the South, hers in many ways is an epic of that South and of cotton mill life in particular.

Mother came to the mills as part of the wave of child laborers in the early years of the 20th century. She was but 12 years old when she pushed a wooden crate up to the machinery at Newry Mill just west of Clemson, South Carolina, in 1924, and she remained a mill hand for more than 52 consecutive years taking breaks only to give birth. Even after retirement, her former bosses at Easley Mill, the plant known formally as the Woodside Division of Dan River Mills, called her back two times before she finally declined their invitation for good. They knew, and shortly you will know, that Mother never met a traveler she could not change.

# Chapter One

## *Learn to Hoe, or Learn to Spin*

In most matters, Mother was not one to complain, and in that there is something remarkable. When my sisters and I were enduring the growing pains of our youth, Mother was never one to point out that she in her childhood had faced far greater difficulties than we. I now know that my childhood grievances would have been trivial by comparison, such as when, with a lot of light left in the day, it was time to leave our friends and our games behind to hurry home for a supper of pinto beans and homemade cornbread, still among my favorite foods.

Had my childhood been as my Mother's was, I might have frequently pointed out to my own children that my formative years were spent in hard labor. Which, in Mother's case, was true, in my case not. Yet, she never made an issue of the fact that at about the age at which I became a Tenderfoot Boy Scout candidate, she worked as many as 10 hours a day at Newry Cotton Mill earning no more than 40 cents a day with which she supported her mother and father, three brothers, a sister and herself.

1

Nor was there much therapeutic value for her in discussing her childhood disadvantages with our mill hill neighbors because she knew that most of those her age also had spent some of their pre-teen and perhaps most of their teenage years sweeping cotton lint from the floors of mills or learning, as she did, the intricacies of running a set of frames in a spinning room.

If anything, the loss of my mother's childhood may well have steeled her determination to see that the three of us had a chance to enjoy ours. It probably is the reason I was encouraged to try everything, so long as there were no morality issues involved and no one was in danger of injury. Living with that sort of freedom in her youth was no option for Mother and thousands like her throughout the South. If she and her contemporaries were not born into slavery, the lives they had in their youth were close to it.

Mother was a part of that wave of child laborers in the first third of the 20th century sent off to the mills by parents eager to keep body and soul together through difficult economic times. Some, we are told, were working in the mills as early as the age of 9. Mother would take a slightly different route. It remains uncertain how much formal education she had though it is likely she attended class very little, if at all, after the second grade. Instead, she remained in the ramshackle house the family called home taking care of younger siblings for her mother whose own commitment to such matters was not admirable. Except for the attention Mother could give them, her young brothers and sister were left most of the time to their own devices, and farm animals, including chickens, wandered in and out of the house at will. Cleanliness was not a priority. Few of the series of sharecropper houses in which the family lived had electricity and none had running water and anything other than crude outdoor toilet facilities.

The appeal of actually working for money in a cotton mill at the age of 12, therefore, was considerable for Mother.

# Come Quittin' Time

While a movement, led by social workers of the day and by newspapers through their reporters and editorial staffs, struggled to make child labor a matter of the public conscience, Mother saw it as an escape. Children in cotton mills and coal mines were dying in the grinding wheels of machinery; others were permanently maimed. It was a chance Mother was willing to take just to escape the squalid conditions of her family home. Her father, an uneducated man himself, did nothing to discourage her decision to seek work in mills instead of pursuing a decent education that, in theory at least, could have been even more liberating.

Mother's thirst for an education, never satisfied, would last a lifetime. She taught herself to read and once she mastered the skill, she never stopped reading. But for her entire lifetime, she was embarrassed by what she saw as a lack of maturity in the undisciplined nature of her own penmanship. It perhaps did not help that she was married to a man with a remarkably beautiful hand when it came to cursive writing. So regrettable to her was her penmanship that she always recruited Dad to sign special occasion cards on her behalf. Just once, she would have loved to have signed a letter to one of us "Mother" written with a perfectly formed 'M'. Even well into her 80s, she still tried to train the muscles in her right arm and hand to the tiny strokes of well-formed cursive letters. She never mastered the art.

Through all the intense practice, her writing would improve only marginally, and the years had long dissolved into history when she might have been a schoolgirl long enough to comfort her in her old age. The day she walked through the doors of the cotton mill at Newry at only 12 years of age, the prospect of an education was gone if, in her family, it ever existed at all. From that point, her working life would be claimed by cotton mills. By the time she retired for the third and last time after twice having been persuaded back to work by bosses desperate for her skills, she had spent more than 52 years as a cotton mill hand. Few people in the history of the industrial revolution that brought cotton manufacturing to the South devoted more time to cotton mills. Like all mill workers of the time, she retired on Social Security and a tiny pension of $11.80 a month for more than a half century of intense, dependable work in the cotton mills of South Carolina. Though Dad's career in the cotton mill was interrupted at least three times when he tried other lines of work, his pension was $35.69 a month, the amount Mother began drawing from the mill when Dad died in 1990.

That Mother felt pressured into adulthood when only a child, first as a care-giver and then as a bread-winner, was perhaps the result of cruel circumstances which she almost never discussed, though the thought must have been there.

Though mired deep in abject poverty for all the time my Mother knew her, her own mother was to the manor born. Named Cleo Tweeter Gibson, she was born on November 30, 1892, to Georgia plantation owners who had considerable land holdings in Rabun County, that picture postcard region tucked against the foot of the Appalachian Mountains in the northern part of the state. Theirs was rich, fertile bottom land that within the lifetime of my grandmother would become some of Georgia's prime resort real estate.

Rabun also was the county where another clan, though not nearly as affluent, was growing in numbers. The Chappells, farmers but not massive landholders, had among their sons Ambrose, 9 years older than Cleo Tweeter.

The Gibson family fortune and the family land already apparently was slipping away when the cute little daughter was born and the shift from wealth to numbing poverty was a rapid one. How it came about remains the subject of family conjecture. The long-accepted explanation is that Grandpa Gibson, the plantation owner and the keeper of the estate, became ill. Doctors from near and far were summoned in an effort to find a cure for whatever was troubling the master of the plantation, until a fortune was gone and all the land had been sold to pay medical bills.

The prevailing theory more recently, however, is that Grandpa Gibson's illness was more addiction than systemic. It is said that he was dealt some hard hands at the poker table and played until he had played himself, his children, and his children's children into poverty from which they would not emerge for more than a generation.

Whatever the legacy, Mother perhaps could not have escaped a difficult childhood, and the question of what might have been is almost certain to have had a devastating effect on the impressionable years in her own mother's life and, indeed, may in part explain her disassociation from normal maternal instincts.

Mother perhaps had no choice but to seek her own place in the world, and given that, cotton mill labor was the most available and convenient escape. Mother's life in a sense paralleled that of the cotton industry in the South. When she was young, the mills were mostly young though there was scattered cotton manufacturing in the South well before the first shot of the Civil War was fired at Fort Sumter. And the numbers grew slowly after the conflict, then with a rush at the dawning of the 20th century, spreading hope as they did for those seeking to join the migration from the farms and the backwoods hills of the South to the new industry of the region. Almost any river or stream with an abundance of moving water sprouted cotton mills through the South. When Mother had grown old, so had the cotton industry and in many cases, including at Easley Mill where she worked most of her life and where we lived, the manufacturing plants withered and died, killed, they said, by imports from foreign countries, principally Japan and China.

By early in the 20th century, though, the boom in the industry was on, bringing with it in some cases the names of far-away places. Newry, a small mill town just west of Clemson University where textile engineering became a major field of study, was named in honor of the town of the same name in Ireland. Among emerging cotton mill communities of the time, Newry was and still is unique. It was a small mill as cotton manufacturing goes, classically built of brick and featuring a tower with Palladium windows as a focal point. Stretching across the hills leading to the mill was the community of unremarkable mill houses. Unlike other cotton manufacturing plants of the time, Newry never attracted the supporting community of banks, clothing and food stores, and other support elements common to most communities. Though its original post office still operates near the old, decaying mill, to call Newry a town is to stretch the definition of the word. There is no town there and the company store closed long before the mill stopped running.

Newry remains an isolated community in Oconee County. The road into Newry also is the favored one out, and many of the houses have long ago fallen into disrepair. The mill stopped humming years ago, and a gallant effort at restoration by some of the former mill hands who live there still is yet to take hold.

But Newry would be the place where Mother would begin her long textile career. It was not far removed from Greenville, South Carolina, just 13 miles east of Easley, which became known for a time as the "textile capital of the world." Among Greenville's cotton manufacturing plants were Judson, Mills Mill, Dunean, Monaghan, Union Bleachery, Woodside, American Spinning, Camperdown, Piedmont, Poinsett, Poe and Brandon where the incomparable and much maligned Shoeless Joe Jackson grew up and to which he returned. Though he had left major league baseball as the disgraced centerpiece of the 1919 Black Sox Scandal, Jackson was welcomed back to his mill hill community as a hero. Such is the loyalty that seems a part of almost all mill hill people. Accusations that he played a key role in the fixing of World Series games, charges that remain controversial long past his death, were never accepted on the streets where Jackson walked, his "black Betsy" bat always at his side. If Joe said it wasn't so, that was good enough for his neighbors at Brandon, one of the "textile crescent" mills on the western side of the growing city of Greenville. Together, the "crescent" mills early in the 20th century employed more than 40,000 people, many of them children, including, in the years before he became a professional baseball player, Joe Jackson who was not yet known as Shoeless.

But if Greenville was growing to support the booming textile industry, Easley came into existence because of it. Spread basically in close proximity to the Southern Railway line that snaked its way through South Carolina's upstate region on its run from Charlotte, North Carolina, to Atlanta, the mills of Easley, coal-fired and not as dependent upon water power as earlier plants, grew to number six - Easley Mill, Glenwood, Alice, Arial, Eljean and Foster, the later the newest and most modern of the lot. In general, they were smaller and therefore employed fewer people than the big factories of Greenville's "textile crescent."

Some modern college lecturers on the subject suggest that child labor in the mills existed mostly from 1900 until about 1920 which, if true, would have excluded Mother. Congress did not enact the Fair Labor Standards Act, the legislation that for the first time established a minimum wage and brought to an end the widespread use of children as laborers not only in cotton mills but in other industrial disciplines, until 1938. By that time, cotton mills in particular had ended their dependence upon children as workers for a variety of social and economic reasons. But Mother was no longer a child.

However, child labor in a much more limited application still existed in the South into World War II. Until the mid-1940s, it was not uncommon for public schools to close for two to three weeks in late October to give students who lived on farms time to help harvest the cotton that grew in fields from near Kannapolis, North Carolina, to Mississippi creating the raw product that fed the many cotton mills. Even mill hill kids, such as I, were encouraged to join the masses laboring in the cotton fields. But for us, it was more recreational than essential. My own limited experience at picking cotton, careful not to slice my fingers on the razor-sharp edges of the open, dry bolls, came in the Oats' fields where I was paid a penny a pound for the cotton I picked.

Still, child labor was in its waning years by the time of the Japanese attack on Pearl Harbor, but not soon enough to make a difference in Mother's life.

Mother was the second oldest of six children born to my grandparents, Ambrose P. and Cleo Tweeter Gibson Chappell, and the eldest, Louise, determined apparently early on with the precise rationale of a child that she wanted no part of cotton mill work. Instead of life as a child laborer, she became a child bride at the age of 13, marrying a much older man who was about to go marching off to fight in World War I. Reputedly a gentle man who worked hard with his hands tilling the soil, Louise's husband, Reuben, came home from war a changed man, mean-spirited and abusive. And the hard edge never went away and the gentle man Louise had known as a child bride seldom appeared again.

Despite the changes in her man, Louise held the marriage together in part by the tenuous thread of religious doctrine that suggested, usually in the strongest of terms, that divorce is no option. Her marriage, thus, was the cross Louise had to bear until Reuben was struck down by a taxi as he crossed Main Street in Greenville soon after the armistice had ended World War II.

The cab's door handle, which protruded perhaps two inches as did most of the era, had impaled Reuben, a large man. He died a day later leaving Louise in the house they had built together along a rural highway in Oconee County and leaving to rust away an array of farm equipment and a large tin shed where he had dabbled in welding.

Louise never remarried, survived three of her four children, and never worked in a cotton mill.

Unlike Louise, for Mother there would be no escaping the mills at so tender an age. The growing Chappell family lived in a tired wooden shack beside a rutted dirt road in Oconee County between Westminster, one of the stops on the busy rail line on which the industry depended, and the Blackjack community. (Later in the century, in keeping with political correctness, Blackjack would become Mount Pleasant). It was to that house that Mother would return every weekend, first by taking a short train ride and then walking the last four to five miles burdened with groceries she had purchased with her earnings at Newry Mill and later as a passenger on a longer train trip from Easley.

Mother had made several such trips home early in her employment at Newry when a Westminster couple living near the railroad tracks began to note the same young girl stepping from the train every Saturday evening burdened with all the groceries she could carry. Finally, the woman sent her husband to inquire if the girl would like to rest a bit before beginning her walk, though they had no idea how far Mother yet had to go.

Within a few weeks, the woman was regularly preparing meals for Mother to enjoy when she disembarked from the train. It was a welcomed break in the tedium of her week for Mother until she accepted an invitation from the woman's husband to drive her home in the truck he had recently purchased. Mother took her place in the passenger seat while the man started the truck, spinning the crank once, twice and then waiting for a moment as the engine coughed and finally chugged to life.

Together they drove across the grade at the railroad tracks, along Main Street which would become part of U.S. Highway 123 between Greenville and Atlanta, and out into the unpaved roads that crisscrossed rural Oconee County. Suddenly, Mother was aware of the man's hand on her knee and she heard him telling her how beautiful she was. Mother's beauty was no exaggeration; in the years ahead, she would be chosen Miss Arial and would represent the Pickens County mill community in the Miss Easley beauty pageant. She now knew what price would be expected for this ride home.

"You stop this truck right now," she ordered and had stepped to the ground almost before the vehicle could be brought to a stop. She removed her groceries from the bed of the truck, thanked the man for the ride and began the long walk home that she by now had made many times before.

She never again acknowledged the couple sitting on the front porch watching passengers step from the train in Westminster and never again joined them for the meal that had been so welcomed.

Still, the long walk home from the train depot would never be easy. For most of the time she made the weekend trips home, she had to walk past a rural farm house from which older men would call to her with invitations so suggestive and frightening that she began to regularly rush at a run past that troublesome spot on her journey, even though loaded down with groceries.

And in the winter months, she had to walk the lonely, frightening country roads frequently in the dark of moonless nights to get her meager collection of groceries to her sharecropper parents and their growing family. Mother eventually, though only briefly, solved the problem by moving her family into a mill house at Newry. There she could watch over her family every day, and there, now removed from the sharecropper fields he had worked in the rural area near Westminster, her father also elected to accept his daughter's generosity. If she was not before, Mother clearly now was her family's lone bread winner.

Even love could not break the shackles that kept Mother in the mills through her teen years. So tethered to the mill was Mother that her first serious flirtation almost ended tragically.

A teenaged co-worker near her age named Wes Ridgeway was among her first suitors. Like Mother, Wes had been pressed into service at Newry Mill when he too was but a child. For a time, the two kept their romance secret for fear, which proved to be justified, that her father might not accept the threat that Mother's pay envelope might no longer come to the family table on a weekly basis.

Grandpa Chappell himself had no simple life. He and grandmother had married when she too was young and cute though Papa, as we called him, could offer little more than a meager living that could be made from the red clay soil of the western tip of South Carolina where he lived for most of his adult life. In another time, he might have been marrying for wealth, but the Gibson wealth of property was no more. Papa himself was a dirt poor dirt farmer who clawed at the rocky red soil so desperately that the regular income represented by Mother's pay envelope seemed a bonanza. Once he moved at Mother's suggestion to Newry, he chose for a time to no longer work the fields.

He, nevertheless, was a possessive man. He already had lost Louise to Reuben and had no intention of losing Mother and her contributions as well. So, when word that Mother had been seen in the company of Wes and that she had accompanied him in his father's truck on a short trip to Seneca for farm supplies, the news triggered a crisis in the four-room mill house Mother had rented and where the family had grown to number six children, two of whom would not survive to adulthood.

Alarmed at the romantic development, Papa determined to do something about the threat to the financial support he gleaned from Mother's labor. In an angry mood, he marched down South Avenue, turned right in front of the mill office and continued down the hill to the factory. He marched into the entrance near the canteen that served sandwiches and soft drinks - known by mill hands as "dopes" - and which offered a brief respite from the sweat-shop conditions on the floors in the era before the advent of air conditioning.

There he found the daughter upon whom he depended and Wes, taking their meal break together and sharing a wooden box as a table. They were talking only loudly enough to each be heard over the roar of the looms and sides clacking and whirling away nearby.

Saying nothing, Papa reached for an empty soft drink bottle and, griping it by the neck, shattered it against the brick wall turning the shards into a deadly weapon with which he attacked Wes.

Wes lay wounded, though not mortally, and the county sheriff dispatched a deputy from the town precinct. My grandfather was arrested and locked away at the county jail at Walhalla.

For hard-working farm hands at the time, his reaction to young love had not been unique, though the violence had been shocking. Wes' parents, who also drew financial support from their own son's cotton mill labors, certainly understood and his mother appeared at the county jail seeking Grandpa Chappell's release.

There was no intention on the part of Wes or his family to press charges, she told the constable. Further, "Mister Chappell has a house full of kids to raise and needs to be out working instead of sitting in jail," she pleaded.

Papa Chappell was released.

Still, he remained opposed to the relationship between his second oldest daughter and the young co-worker, and made no secret of his concern. It was an opposition to love which both Mother and Wes understood so well that when Wes walked Mother home one Saturday evening, the two stopped to talk softly beneath a tree not far from the front porch of the Chappell mill hill home. As a young man in love is likely to do, Wes drew Mother close and the two kissed goodnight.

The kiss had barely ended when fear that her fiery father had seen the embrace griped both teenagers. If he had, how would he react? Would he punish Mother, and if he did, how violent would the punishment be? Wes certainly understood how violent the man could be and had healing wounds as reminders.

"I sleep in that room," Mother said, speaking secretively and pointing to a window in the house that was a duplicate of Wes' own home less than 100 yards away. "I'll go in and turn on the light and get ready for bed. The light should go out in a few minutes if everything's OK. If it stays on ..."

"I know," Wes answered softly. "I'll be right here."

Mother turned and as quietly as possible climbed the steps to the front porch. She knew that the weathered old floor boards would creak with each step. Still, she moved slowly, trying to walk softly, and finally she disappeared from Wes' view inside the house.

The light in the window to which Mother had pointed came on. Wes waited, watching the glow of that single light for what seemed too long. Finally, the room went dark. Wes lingered briefly, listening, hearing nothing but the raspy creaking of the tree frogs and an old hound dog barking in the distance. It wasn't one-if-by-land-and-two-if-by-sea, but the turning off of the light apparently meant that all was well and that there would be no violent price to pay on this night for a summer kiss shared beneath a spreading tree.

# Chapter Two

## *A Depression to Last a Lifetime*

Wes was in Mother's life prior to the time the Great Depression was ravaging the country. When the Wall Street crash of October 29, 1929 came, the textile industry had been in a period of robust growth in the South despite the major issues it faced, including the philosophy of child labor and the length of a day's work. South Carolina was unique among the states in addressing, at least in a token manner, the issue of child labor. Palmetto State legislators early in the century had passed a law that prohibited children younger than 10 from working in cotton mills. And the state had sought, with uneven success, to limit the definition of a "working day" for all workers, but specifically for children.

The measures were not completely successful. It was not uncommon for children younger than 10 to be employed as doffer boys and such throughout the South, and when inspectors from the state arrived on site, word would spread quickly through the mill sending children scurrying for hiding places. For fear of losing their jobs, the children remained voluntarily secreted away in closets and large boxes until the inspectors, satisfied that the mill was in compliance, had left.

Because of her advanced age of 12, Mother was spared such a clandestine existence.

By the time Mother joined the textile labor force in 1924, a 66-hour week had become standard for mill workers throughout the South - 12 hours a day for five days and a half day, or six hours, on Saturdays. The 12-hour day was a holdover from farm life where the work of a day was considered to be from sunup to sundown, or about a dozen hours. The rationale was that the migrating agricultural workers, who were rapidly becoming the backbone of the cotton manufacturing industry, were accustomed to such hours and the long day would seem a realistic expectation. But that theory took no consideration of breaks forced on the farms by bad weather, or shorter winter work days.

All of that began to change with the Great Depression when some cotton mills, operating on thin capitalization even in good times, closed permanently as did many different kinds of industry across America. Yet, the textile industry overall weathered the downturn in fortunes better than some other industries through curtailing. Limiting operations to two and three days per week became commonplace and few textile workers were left completely without work and a source of income. Some mill owners also arranged extensions of credit in company stores as a way of helping families through the Depression.

For Mother and her family, the resounding shock waves of the crash on Wall Street was more annoyance than catastrophe for one simple reason: For the Chappells and thousands of sharecroppers like them, their Great Depression had been going on for generations, certainly since the Civil War and the post-conflict dissolution of the agrarian South built in part on plantation life. For many white Southerners, including the

Chappell clan, the loss of the pre-Civil War farming economy was a greater blow than the arrival of the Great Depression. Those who had worked on the plantations frequently saw no escape from the collapse of their way of life except by turning to sharecropping.

Except for the times he lived briefly in houses on or near mill hills, rented by Mother, Papa Chappell was a sharecropper, a man left to the whims of weather and cutworms, for almost all his life from about 1890 when he was only seven until he died in 1950. He was the head of a household who went from one small- to medium-sized farm to another hoping to make a farming deal for the next planting season, and for whom any shack was shelter in the economic storms he constantly faced.

So, the Great Depression of history, which arrived when Mother was 17 and already a skilled mill hand, caused barely a ripple in the Chappell household which by late in 1929 had moved from Newry and back to the hard fields of Oconee County. Papa had returned to scratching gnarly potatoes, a bit of corn and a few runners of beans from the soil; if anything, life was marginally better because the family now had Mother's pay envelope, meager though it was, to help them through the hard times that kept coming like an endless freight train. Papa's livelihood was never based upon cash, but upon the barter system, and he perhaps never actually saw as much as $200 in any context in the course of a year. Papa lost nothing during the crash because he never had money to invest and the closest Great Depression soup line was hundreds of miles away. His own economic base, if there had ever been one, had collapsed far earlier.

Hard times were simply a daily part of life. The growing Chappell family already had survived the great influenza pandemic of 1917 and 1918 that ravaged the world, including many of the farming families across the South. On our father's side of the Browning family, tombstones on graves of ancestors who died of the flu on their Georgia farms bear witness to the scourge that claimed between 2 and 4 million lives worldwide and which was more devastating globally than the great plagues of Europe earlier.

But Mother had survived along with her parents and all her siblings.

The romance with Wes never developed beyond teenage love. Still, when his obituary appeared in newspapers in the South Carolina upstate sometime in the decade of the 1990s, Mother wept softly for her long-ago love.

There is no doubt that Mother took her financial responsibility to her family seriously. But what her childhood employment had accomplished was to remove her from the succession of dirty, barely inhabitable sharecropper shacks, most without electricity in a time when electrification still was new and considered a luxury even in cities and towns, and none with indoor plumbing. Still, when Mother picked up her pay envelope every Friday, she would spend a portion of it at a community grocery, board a train with the food she had purchased and travel from Newry to Westminster to deliver the goods and most of her remaining week's pay to her parents, keeping only enough to provide meager room and board for herself.

Though Mother had not yet met our father, Dad's life at the time was similar to that of Mother's in that he also worked to help support a large mill hill family. But there were great contrasts as well. Dad remained in school through the eighth grade, then as the eldest of six sons and a daughter he too took his place as a mill hand at Glenwood Mill at Easley. For Dad, it seemed a natural progression. Both his mother and father were raised on Georgia farms and early in the 20th century had joined that massive migration from the farm fields to the cotton mills. And unlike Mother's parents, Dad's mother and father also worked in the mill.

Dad's living conditions as a teenager also were in sharp contrast to those Mother faced. His home was on Turner Street at Glenwood Mill, a four-room house that was kept virtually pristine clean. Out back, there was a garden, but no chickens wandering into and out of the house, and no farm animals. A huge fig tree grew at the corner of the frame house providing the fruit for jams to spread on cold winter days on wonderful homemade biscuits. All of the two-hole outhouses were installed near the back of the yards in the neighborhood and there were clean slop pails placed beneath each bed in the event nature called in the dark of night. It was an easy walk to work for Dad and his parents who at one time even had owned a Model T. Dad faithfully delivered his unopened pay envelop each week to his mother. She, in turn, gave Dad a modest allowance to last him until the next payday.

For the Chappells, the nearest neighbor might be another sharecropper a mile away along deeply rutted country dirt roads. Dad's family lived in the Glenwood Mill community. Papa Browning's sister, Aunt Emma, lived nearby as did his brother Fred. The Hudson family lived across the alley at the back, and the house directly opposite on Turner Street was the home of the McNeelys. Ervin McNeely, the head of the household, worked in the mill as well and also drove "McNeely's Jitney" offering, for a modest fee, regular transportation to and from town only three miles away. And on the still of a summer day, with all the windows to the homes open to welcome any cooling breeze, the sweet sounds of Mr. McNeely's trumpet could be heard as he practiced his assignments, mostly Sousa, for the mill village's brass band.

Among his children was a beautiful daughter named Jessie Lee who would become my aunt, the bride of one of Dad's younger brothers, Clarence.

The first time I left home with anyone not named Browning was in the company of Mr. McNeely who in the summer of 1940, when I was only three, invited me to join him in his Model A Ford for a trip to "big Greenville." But it was the trumpet that drew me in my pre-school enthusiasm to Mr. McNeely. He was the reason I chose, in my turn, to play the instrument at the high school level. And because there always was an old trumpet laying around our home, our youngest son, Andrew, also chose the b-flat brass and became a far more accomplished performer than I.

Today, Andrew is a band director in Davidson County, North Carolina, and thus brings new students to band music every year, perhaps without ever pausing to consider the legacy his work represents for an old mill village trumpet player.

Mr. McNeely would be pleased and perhaps surprised that his influence continues long past his death.


The contrast between the Browning household and that of the Chappells was remarkable and came to underscore the difference in a family fully committed to the new industry of the South, cotton manufacturing, and a family still of the red clay soil of the South Carolina Upstate.

Mother needed no college degree to understand that leaving home to work in a cotton mill had brought dramatic changes in her own life and it is clear that she never intended to return to the life of sharecropping on a permanent basis. For as long as her own mother and father would live, however, she would do what she could to see to their well-being.

At Newry as a young girl barely into her teen years, Mother faced one profound change in her life after another. Not only was Wes in her life as her first serious boyfriend, but she was taking more and more interest in the religious part of her life as well. More and more frequently now, she was making excuses to her mother and father that she needed to cut her weekend visits short to return to Newry. The fact that she was drawn to the Baptist Church was not mentioned for fear that

that also would be seen by her parents as yet another step away from home for the one member of the family who could be counted upon.

Indeed, when Mother asked to be baptized into the Baptist Church, the emersion took place before a congregation made up almost entirely of people she had not known a year earlier and in the mill hill's Union Church, which meant it was shared by both Baptists and Methodists on alternating Sundays. On the day of her baptism, there was no kin in the congregation to offer support for Mother or to serve as witnesses.

Baptism was nothing new to Mother. As a young girl, before the weight of the work-a-day world descended upon her, she found a cluster of equally young friends, also the children of sharecroppers, in whose company she spent long summer hours. One of the young boys must have been a budding minister, she once said. He frequently would suggest that the group "play preacher and do some baptizing." Together they would make their way to a nearby stream where, because she was the smallest child in the group, Mother was the most frequent baptism recipient.

Later in her life, she also joined one of her grandsons, Thomas Burke, when he was baptized into the family church in Easley. All in all, Mother felt that she should have been listed in the Guinness record book as the most baptized person in the world.

All the water did not wash away nor even dampen Mother's spirit. It came as something of a shock to her family when she confirmed late in her life that during the massive attempts to bring the textile industry into organized labor, Mother had been one of only seven people at Easley Mill who voted in favor of union representation. Dad voted against the union. But Mother, even at a very young age, had not been inadequate in representing herself. Since as a teenager hers was the only pay envelope from the cotton mills to reach the family table in the Chappell household, Mother felt the pressure of being the family's only bread-winner.

On one particularly stressful day, the determined teenager marched off her job at Newry and into the office of the mill superintendent which, in itself, represented a bit of daring. A mill superintendent throughout the first half of the 20th century was a remarkably powerful man in the lives of mill hands. Not only was he the man who had primary responsibility for the smooth operation of cloth manufacturing, he also frequently served as a one-man judge and jury. He had the power to summarily evict mill house renters without appeal, and he was the man who settled all disputes among neighbors.

Local police were almost never called to resolve incidents on the mill hill. Instead, it was the superintendent - called, appropriately, "the super" - who handled such matters. In the late 1940s, for example, when my father was unable to persuade a group of young adults to stop hitting baseballs in the direction of our house, he took his grievance not to the local police, but to the ultimate authority, the super. The baseballs stopped raining on our house before Dad had returned home from the super's office at the mill. And they never came again.

It, thus, was with more than a dash of daring that Mother arrived unannounced at the super's office at Newry with a complaint. She knew that her immediate supervisor on the floor would have no authority to address her grievance and, had she chosen that route, she understood as well that it would take days for a response to be passed back down the chain of command from the super. She, therefore, had gone directly to the top.

"My name is Martha Chappell," she announced as she stood before the man who was seated behind a huge desk in his wood-paneled office, the smell of cigar smoke hanging heavy in the air.

"Martha Chappell," he took note.

21

"Yes, sir. And I've come here to tell you I need more money. I have a mother and dad and a sister and three brothers at home to support. I'm the only one in my family bringing home a pay envelope. Now, I work hard for you. I'm always on time and I never miss a shift and I think I deserve a raise."

"What'd you have in mind?" the super asked.

"Maybe five dollars more a week. $35 instead of $30."

"You've got it," the super said. "But Martha, let's just keep this between the two of us."

Mother kept it just between the two of them for more than 70 years.

# Chapter Three

## *Hard Times, Good Times*

It was the Great Depression, and the drastically reduced working schedule at Newry following that national calamity that signaled the next big change in Mother's young life. Still little more than a child herself, Mother reasoned that if there were economic shelter from the Wall Street disaster, it would be found in Easley, South Carolina. There, A. Foster McKissick and Ellison S. McKissick, father and son, had purchased the 13-year-old Alice Manufacturing plant in 1923 and by 1926 had doubled its capacity on the way to a textile empire that would eventually include five mills in Easley alone.

Remarkably, despite the gathering economic storm clouds, Ellison S. McKissick also had built a new mill, Arial, a mere two miles from Alice Manufacturing and began making cotton cloth in 1928. He, thus, had created a boom town at a time when bread and soup lines were forming in other parts of the country, and despite the news that some of the big losers on Wall Street were said to be committing suicide. Despite the Depression, McKissick needed experienced mill hands to make the new machinery work, and had the money to pay them. Mother, then 18, was among the first wave of workers at the new plant, leaving her beloved church and Wes behind and moving to Pickens County. Though she, of course, did not know it at the time, it would become her home for the rest of her life. When Mother became one of two boarders in Lyda Underwood's home near the Arial Mill village, which still was under construction, the very horizons of her world seemed to have expanded. And the sharecropper shack, where the Chappells lived in Oconee County, was even further away both figuratively and literally.

Mrs. Underwood herself was then barely beyond her teen years and newly married when Mother arrived at her house as a boarder. Not much older than Mother, Mrs. Underwood became a friend and mentor and dramatically changed Mother's life forever. It was in the Underwood home that Mother learned the lifetime skills her own mother had neither taught nor practiced.

Mrs. Underwood taught Mother the importance of cleanliness in the home, and that there was a place for everything and everything should be in its place. She was such a taskmaster that she would regularly inspect even the most remote corners for any signs of dust or dirt. Mother and another young woman boarder learned to work together to the point that in their daily cleanings one would lift one end of the sofa while the other cleaned the floor beneath. Then they would repeat the process at the other end. And each time it happened, Mother felt a disquieting ache deep inside.

It also was Mrs. Underwood who taught Mother the fine points of sewing in a time when American laborers frequently made their own clothing, often from the cloth of flour sacks. Mother became an expert at the craft and in the half century that lay ahead would not only create clothing for her family, but regularly make aprons for other women who worked in the mill. By the late 1940s and through the 1970s, Mother's aprons were in high demand and sold for as much as $2.50 each, an astonishing price at the time.

But Mrs. Underwood had more to teach in those Depression years. As her student, Mother also learned etiquette and good manners, and such niceties as whether the knife and spoon should be placed on a specific side of a dinner plate opposite the dinner fork, fine points that had held no importance in her childhood home. Even the names of meals were fine-tuned by Mrs. Underwood. For years, mill workers referred to the noon meal as "dinner," and the evening meal as "supper." Without abandoning the tradition entirely, Mother also knew that it was, more properly, "lunch" and "dinner."

In all, they were lessons that Mother would honor for as long as she lived, and she honored Mrs. Underwood for changing her life in a profound way by sending her fresh homemade pies regularly, even in the final year of Mother's life.

One thing that did not change, however, was Mother's weekly ritual of buying groceries and traveling to the shack the rest of her family called home. She still made the trip by train, but now the journey was longer and her burden of groceries no lighter, the late-day summer heat of her long Friday walks from the train station to her parents' home no more pleasant, nor the dark winter evenings no less chilling.

The distance that lay between that Oconee County shack and Arial Mill, in both miles and life style, now was greater than ever. But Mother's new life did not represent a change so profound that it could diminish in any way her feelings of accountability when it came to the squalid existence of her immediate family. Long before she had reached her teen years, when she was no more than 8, Mother had dropped out of school to take on the role and responsibilities of homemaker in the Chappell house, a role her own mother had long ago abdicated if, indeed, she had ever accepted such responsibility in the first place.

The years of child labor in the cotton mills had in part taken her away from that, but had not erased her feelings of responsibility in that regard. Mother's world had expanded from one county to two counties, but she could not emotionally escape the shack near Westminster.

Louise had long ago married the older, harsh Reubin and seldom returned to any of the series of rundown houses the Chappells called home, though most of the time she lived less than 10 miles away. And Lula, the younger of Mother's two sisters, was now a teenager herself and, like Louise, also not inclined to assume the mountain of responsibility that should have been their mother's.

Those weekend trips home were taking their toll. And Mother, now in her late teens, made yet another adult decision. Blessed with steady work in a time of national crisis, she rented a home on the hill near where radio station WELP now operates, and once again moved her family closer to her work so she could watch over them seven days a week instead of on weekends only.

If Mother's world had expanded by one county, so had her list of friends and acquaintances grown longer. Mother thought about Wes from time to time, and wondered how he was doing so far away now in Newry. But she had other friends now, though not yet one to replace Wes. Dora Roach, a girl about her age, also worked at Arial Mill and had become one of Mother's pals, though a jealousy arose between the Roach sisters, Dora and her younger sibling, Amanda.

Amanda apparently saw in Mother a rare beauty and had wanted to be among Mother's small circle of friends. It was such an attraction that Amanda once prevented Dora from having an evening out with Mother and several other friends by hiding

Dora's favorite shoes until it was too late for Dora to join the group.

"I hated Dora," Amanda confessed years later. "I wanted to be Martha's friend."

Mother apparently had little time with her mill work and taking care of her family to note the sibling rivalry between Amanda and Dora. When Mother was chosen to represent the Arial community in the Miss Easley beauty pageant, Amanda's opinion of Mother and her striking appearance was confirmed.

But Dora would come to have a far more important role in Mother's life than that of a friend only.

Many members of the large Roach family, with its various branches in the community, regularly attended the young, growing Easley Church of God, a congregation in which my Father's mother had been a founding member, as had the elders in the Roach family. Through the early years, church services were held in the homes of various members and the Roach family had been among the most prominent of those. So, the Roach sisters, Dora and Amanda, already were acquainted with Dad through his attendance at church. He too was a mill hand, working his regular shift at Glenwood Mill on the eastern side of the growing town from Arial, which was then one of two mills in Easley belonging to the McKissicks.

Dad, known as "Bill" to many of his friends, was three years younger than Mother. Like Mother, Dad's parents had known the hard work and the hard times of work on the farm in Georgia. Unlike Mother's parents, when new cotton manufacturing plants began springing up throughout the South, Dad's parents made a decision that would differ dramatically from that of the Chappells. As a couple, they left the farm, as did thousands like them, and became among the first of the Southern mill hands.

Methodist for all his life, my grandfather did not share his wife's enthusiasm for membership in the fledgling Church of

God in Easley, but he supported her completely. For many weeks, services for the new church were held in the Browning's front yard on Turner Street at Glenwood, on benches my Dad's father had erected. And it was he who constructed the first pews used in the church, though he had to walk to and from the lumber yard carrying three hand-chosen boards per trip until he had enough wood to build seating for a modest congregation.

While my grandfather was never an active member of the Church of God, he never discouraged his wife's commitment. Indeed, for as long as he lived, when a new minister was assigned to the congregation, one of the first people he met was my grandfather who insisted upon joining the newly arrived parson on a trip to town where Grandfather Browning always bought the new pastor a new hat.

Both of my father's parents were born and raised in the Hartwell-Royston section of northeast Georgia, but moved to the South Carolina Upstate where cotton mills seemed to be going up all along the rail lines and river systems. Together, they brought home a comfortable living for the times and, for a time, even owned an automobile, a rare possession on the early mill hills. And for a time, Dad's father drove the car.

It was from his father that Dad got his strong, quiet outlook on life, and much of his determination. That determination was never demonstrated more pointedly than the day Dad's mother and father were motoring through the countryside near Easley and his father came close to missing a turn.

"I thought you were going to turn here," Dad's mother said to her husband who was at the wheel.

"I am," he grumbled. And with that he pulled the steering wheel hard to the left, missed the turn and came to a stop in a cotton field.

He stepped from the car, walked home and never drove again.

For the rest of his life, our paternal grandfather walked almost everywhere he went. Even into retirement, he walked the six miles round trip almost every day from his home at Glenwood Mill to downtown Easley. And having grown lonesome for his wife when she made a trip to Hartwell once to visit relatives, he walked from Easley to the northeast Georgia town to be with her.

Later in life, he laughed about his final driving experience in his Model T, for his was a gentle humor with which he would delight his grandchildren in years to come by telling and retelling the same stories.

"Me and three of my brothers went down to the river to do some fishing one time down in Georgia," he would always begin. "When we got to the river, there was a 60-year-old man fishing where we wanted to fish."

"What did you do?" one of us would always ask.

"Well, sir. We beat him up."

"You beat up a 60-year old man?"

"Sure did," he would grin. "I think we could have beat him up if he'd been 80."

Nobody laughed at the old worn jokes more than he, nor was there anyone who wanted to hear them again and again more than his grandchildren.

While there was seldom a show of fondness between Mother's parents, Dad's parents remained obviously in love for more than 60 years. On April 28, 1975, at the age of 89, Dad's father called gently in the night to his wife.

"Come lay with me for a while," he said.

She drew back a part of the covers on his bed and lay close to him once again, snuggling to his shoulder. He hugged her to his side. "You've always been my sweetheart," he said to her.

"Sure have," she agreed.

He sighed.

Then he died.

That was the stock from which Dad, the oldest of five sons and a daughter, had sprung. Though he could trace his own roots to the red clay of Georgia, Dad had a certain continental look about him as a late teenager and young adult. He was not a large man, but strongly built, with coal black hair with just enough unruliness to be interesting. He combed his hair straight back, though not severely.

Like his father, he was regarded as a quiet man, more a listener than a speaker, but with such inner strength even as a child that he never wept on those rare occasions when he was spanked. He carried near the elbow of his right arm for most of his life a scar the size of a softball where scalding coffee once was spilled. Even against the agonizing pain of the burn, his mother said, he had not wept.

Dad was considered to be almost as handsome as Mother was beautiful, and in the eyes of Dora would be the perfect date for Mother if only briefly. In order to test her matchmaking skills, Dora invited Mother to her church. There, she pointed out the young man with the chiseled features, and Mother agreed to an introduction.

Instead, Dora arranged a double date - Dora and Bill Griffith, the man she would marry, and Martha Chappell and Willie Lee Browning, aka Bill. Mother was never known to have used Dad's nickname, though through most of his life Dad signed cards to mother as either "Bill" or "W.L."

Dora's efforts at matchmaking almost collapsed before they began.

Friday, April 1, 1932, had been one of those perfect spring days, a warming sun bringing assurance that winter was past, the hillsides near Arial Mill turning a dozen hues of green in their transformations, a freshness in the air that comes only with the new season. And perhaps even a hint of romance.

Mother had hurried to purchase groceries when her shift at Arial Mill had ended earlier in the day, and had wasted little time in seeing to her family. Then she hurriedly got ready for the first real date she had had since leaving Wes behind at Newry.

It had been a busy week. She worked her usual full shifts, and had accompanied Amanda and Dora to a revival that had been running all week at the Church of God, and which still had a week to go. An evangelist had come from out of town to preach every evening and a pretty young lady had accompanied him as the pianist. The young church did not yet have a parsonage so that it could offer convenient living arrangements for visiting preachers and musicians. Instead, various members were to open their homes to the visitors.

For the first week of the revival, the young lady piano player had been a guest in Dad's home, invited there by his mother, already one of the pillars of the church. Near the end of the first week, it fell Dad's lot to deliver the pianist to the home where she would live through the second week of services. So he too was in a rush as the hour of the double date with Mother, Dora and Bill approached.

Mother pushed the creaking porch swing softly back and forth as she waited and when she heard the sound of an approaching automobile as it made the turn off the Pickens Highway, she waited for the car to come into view. When she was certain that it was the Model T Ford that belonged to the Brownings, she stood, pushed the soft wrinkles from her freshly ironed dress and moved to the top step.

She was about to wave when she realized that the car apparently was not going to stop. Indeed, it sped past where Mother stood and not 20 feet from the bottom step to her front porch. It unmistakably was Willie Lee Browning at the wheel. But there in the passenger seat was the pretty piano player. Mother did not know that the cute visitor was being delivered to the home of a member of the church not far from where the Chappells now lived. She knew only what she had seen.

For Mother, it was not a good beginning to a possible relationship. By the time Dad returned to the Chappell house, Mother had retreated to her room and out of sight. And her mother, who had answered Dad's knocking at the door, had seemed less than cordial.

It required more than a little explaining for Mother to agree to participate in the double date which, at best, now seemed not destined to blossom like a spring flower.

But Willie Lee and Martha made a handsome couple, as Dora knew they would, and romance indeed blossomed. For both, life seemed good. The Great Depression had given way to great hope in their own lives.

More and more, Dad was the center of most of Mother's free time though he himself stayed busy not only as a mill hand at Glenwood, but serving as a truck driver for Mr. Ponder who owned the ice cream parlor on East Main Street in Easley.

To this day and for more than 100 years, dating teenagers have been drawn to the ice cream parlor which today is known simply as "Joe's." It is the home not only of an array of ice cream flavors, but chili hot dogs and the best chili and onion hamburgers in that part of South Carolina. When Willie Lee and Martha were dating, it also featured floors covered regularly in fresh saw mill shavings, and a juke box that always was filled with current favorites.

It was seldom available, however, for private parties. But on one memorable evening in the early 1930s, it became the private domain of the two people who would become our parents.

"Bill," Mr. Ponder had informed Willie Lee when he arrived for his second job late one afternoon, "I need for you to take the truck and go to Greenville to pick up supplies.

"Why don't you take that pretty girl that you've been seeing with you? We'll be closed when you get back but take a key and let yourself in, put the supplies away and then enjoy all the ice cream the two of you want."

Late that evening with his chores done, Willie Lee found a way to turn down the volume on the juke box machine and he and the girl with whom he had fallen in love chose a booth, talked into the night and ate ice cream.

It may have been the most important of evenings for the three Browning children who were yet to be born. Among the keepsakes found among Mother's personal possessions following her death was a small wooden ice cream spoon. On it was written in Dad's clear, steady hand "Martha and Bill, April 1, 1932."

# Chapter Four

## *Good Times, Sad Times*

If anyone on the mill hill did more walking than Papa Browning, it would have been the Glenwood Baptist Church pastor, Rev. J.S. Graham. Preacher Graham led the growing congregation longer than any man in the first half of the 20$^{th}$ century, and during the 1930s could be seen daily walking virtually every street that made up the Glenwood Mill village, crisscrossing the neighborhood from Mayes Street on the west side of the community to Powell Street on the east.

Though he regularly visited and prayed for the sick, Preacher Graham perhaps knew more mill hands and their children by their first names than anyone in the community, whether they were members of his church or not.

It was not uncommon, for example, for the parson to visit on a sunny day with Aunt Emma Glover as she hung her wash on the line beside her house near the intersection of Turner Street and Saluda Dam Road, or to stop by to chat a bit with Mr. McNeely. He might even rub the head of little George Pitts and offer a bit of penny candy as he passed along Blue Ridge

Street. The preacher would wander into the barbershop beside the general store on Hagood Street even when he already had a fresh trim. There he would join in conversation about what was happening in Europe, how the sides were running in the mill nearby, or whether the mill baseball team could use another pitcher.

One of the people he came to know on a first-name basis in this manner was the man who would become my Dad, so that Dad saw him as a friend. Though Dad was active in the Church of God and, despite his youth, was an administrator in the church, one of the first people outside the family to know that Mother had accepted Dad's proposal of marriage was Preacher Graham.

"I know I'm not one of your members," Dad said to the preacher, "but I was wondering if you'd do our wedding."

"Sure, I would," Preacher Graham agreed, shaking Dad's hand as he did. "Where's the wedding going to be?"

"We're not sure yet," Dad answered. "You know, our church still meets in the store building in town. We could get married there, but we're still thinking about it."

"Why don't you get married in our parsonage?" Preacher Graham suggested, offering his own home.

And so, on Christmas Eve, 1934, Dora's matchmaking skills were confirmed. Dora and her new husband Bill Griffith were there in the Glenwood Baptist Church parsonage's living room to serve as witnesses when Preacher Graham pronounced the two to be man and wife. Mother was 22 years old, Dad 19. They made a handsome couple.

None of us kids, of course, was there. But in the coming years each of us could imagine Dad holding Mother close when it was time to kiss the bride and, with that hint of a smile, looking deeply into her eyes, saying nothing. It was the embrace the three of us came to know between our parents for years, and the older we became the more meaningful were those unspoken words between our parents. To the two of them, it perhaps was merely a close embrace. To us, it was the look of love, deep and abiding. And though only children, we knew how lucky we were. That first kiss as husband and wife must have been of that sort.

Once the ceremony had been completed, and the bride had been kissed, the two newlyweds did not drive off into the sunset to begin their life together, and cruises then were only for the very wealthy, which excluded the two of them. Instead, they drove once again up the hill to the Browning home on Turner Street where they spent their first night as Mr. and Mrs. Willie Lee Browning.

Happy times and difficult times lay ahead. For Dad, it was the end of regularly delivering his pay envelop to his own mother and accepting an allowance to last him the week. Now, his pay - all of it - would go to his needs and those of his new bride.

Mother, on the other hand, continued to, on a reduced basis, look after the needs of her parents who were still living in the house she had rented on the hill near the Arial Mill village. Marriage could not absolve her of that responsibility, nor would she for as long as she would live escape the inclination to serve as a parent to her parents, even after her own marriage and even beyond her mother's old age.

Soon after the marriage ceremony, Mother left her job and her friends at Arial Mill behind and went to work at Glenwood where Dad had been employed for five years. Though the first few days of their marriage were spent in the Browning home on Turner Street, they soon rented three rooms in a duplex on Northeast Main Street near Easley's commercial center. The two had to walk a mile or more one way to Glenwood Mill, but the duplex was across the railroad tracks and within two blocks of Ponder's Ice Cream Parlor where Dad still worked on a part-time basis driving a truck and gathering supplies. To Mother's and Dad's half of the duplex, a bathroom had been added, though to reach it the newlyweds had to walk across an open back porch. It was there in the bathroom that a lavatory had been placed just below a window where Mother regularly prepared for bed, until the evening that she looked up from washing her face. She intended to look into the gathering darkness of the night beyond the window and to the few lights visible in the neighborhood. Instead, she looked into the face of a man she did not know looking back at her.

It was a moment far more frightening than the fleeting instances in those long walks home alone on the dark of winter nights, when she made the trek from the train depot at Westminster to the house where her waiting parents lived. On those dark walks, she knew that any movement among the swaying pines beside the rutted dirt road fired her imagination, causing her heart to race from fear. But she understood that those frightening moments were mostly only of her imagination. But this was different. This monster that looked back at her from beyond the window had a face, and frightening eyes. This man who was intruding into her world was not of her imagination, but real. For the rest of the short time the couple lived there, shades would be tightly drawn, and Dad regularly searched the generous yard each night before Mother would prepare for her rest.

Lula, Mother's younger sister, also was well into her teen years at the time of the marriage. Since moving with the rest of her family to live with Mother in the house on the hill and across the railroad tracks from Arial Mill, Lula had gathered about her a new group of friends as well. The town of Easley lay a mere three miles away, an easy walk for Lula and some of her friends in an era long before every teenager had access to an automobile.

Lula had been on such a trip with one of her girlfriends that Wednesday, September 25, 1935, and was expected home at almost any time as the Chappells sat down for their last meager meal of the day. The autumn sun was sinking low in the western sky and the shadows had grown long.

Lula would never make it home.

Talking as they walked side-by-side along the highway connecting Easley and Pickens, Lula and her friend had just reached the crest of the long hill leading up to the Arial Mill village when Lula, closest to the road, was struck by a hit-and-run motorist. She died instantly. The identity of the driver has never been determined, though members of the family carried with them for as long as they lived haunting suspicions centered around a certain car that until that fateful day had roared past their house every evening. Once Lula died, the mysterious car came no more. Because law enforcement officers were unable to conclusively identify the driver of the car that struck Lula, there also was never a resolution for the most important question of all:

Was it an accident, or was it murder?

Lula, only 17 years old, had died so close to home that, though her mother and father and younger brother, William, could not have seen what happened, they heard the sickening, deadly impact, a chilling sound locked into their memories for as long as they would live..

Within a year, the Chappells returned without two of their daughters, Mother and Lula, to the sharecropper shacks of Oconee County. Only William, the youngest of six siblings, remained in the nest. Frank, the oldest of three brothers, soon would be married and Morris, the middle son, already was away living on his own, a wanderer returning home only as his own difficult circumstances dictated.

For the rest of her life, Mother kept among her most precious reminders of her sister a lock of Lula's auburn hair.

Following Lula's death, with her parents having returned to the dirt farms of Oconee County, Mother no longer made the trip to Westminster on weekends as frequently as she had for most of her teenage years. And once again her father returned to scratching at the hard, red Upstate South Carolina clay for barely enough to feed the three of them.

A newlywed, Dad continued to labor in the slasher room at Glenwood Mill, one of the hottest and most humid of work areas along the way in transforming raw, ginned cotton into broadcloth. And the seemingly incessant heat was taking its toll on the young married man.

But Mother was suffering recurring health problems of her own, that aching feeling deep inside that she first had noticed again and again as she hefted an end of Mrs. Underwood's couch as part of her regular cleaning chores with her roommate when she lived near Arial. The ache, while bearable, was finally troubling enough to send mother to the family physician, Dr. Cutchens.

"At some time in the past, you've lifted something rather heavy," Dr. Cutchens said to Mother soon after he had examined her. "You seem to have some internal damage, probably caused by heavy lifting."

"Well, almost every day, I used to lift the end of a couch so we could sweep under it," she remembered.

Dr. Cutchens doubted that the weight of the end of a sofa, while heavy, would cause such damage in someone as otherwise healthy as Mother seemed to be. Then she remembered her boarding days at Newry Mill. There, in order to defray some of the boarding costs, thus leaving more money to spend on groceries to deliver to her mother and father, she had helped care for an elderly lady, the mother of the woman who ran the boarding house. The woman was large, and an invalid, and it was Mother's duty to lift her into bed and to move her for bathing from time to time. It had been almost more than Mother could manage.

"That would do it," Dr. Cutchens offered.

The injury, he said, was something Mother could live with, though without surgery to correct the condition she could never have children. A year into her marriage, Mother would submit to the surgery. And by the time they moved to a two-story house on Powell Street, just off the mill hill at Glenwood, she was pregnant with me.

As I understand it, I did not come gently into the world. Mother's labor, intense as it usually is, lasted several days. Dad and his mother tried to make it all bearable for Mother, but nothing seemed to help and the pain came again and again.

Two days before the birth, with Mother in great distress, Mama Browning made the short two-block walk from her home on Turner Street to Mother's bedside in the house on Powell Street. She brought with her a well-sharpened ax.

"Let Willie Lee put this ax under your bed," Mama Browning suggested. "It'll cut the pain."

Dutifully, Dad slid the ax with the gleaming, sharp blade - with the blade pointed up in keeping with his mother's directions - beneath the bed where Mother lay in agony. Whether honoring the superstition made the labor pain more bearable for Mother is not clear. What seems more certain now is that our grandmother was a woman of two worlds; her Christian faith was profound, yet she also kept one foot in the superstitious world of rural Georgia where she grew up. She probably tossed more salt over her shoulder, for good luck, than most people taste in a lifetime.

Whatever Dad's mother contributed to the event of my birth, Mother survived the agony. My own survival was less certain. If the pregnancy had been difficult for Mother, it also had been no picnic for me. When I arrived on June 11, 1937, I am told, I was in less than robust health. Within hours I would develop double pneumonia and my new skill of merely breathing became alarmingly labored and shallow. Dr. Cutchens, who had attended the at-home birth, told the young couple and Mama

Browning that my chances of surviving more than a few days were small indeed. He said that already, I lay close to death.

My grandmother took the ax from beneath the bed and walked home. When she put the ax away, she temporarily stored her superstitions as well. Retreating to the bedroom she shared with my grandfather, she prayed for my survival. When she was finished, she arose and walked once again down Turner Street and turned right onto Powell, a route she had taken many times in recent days.

She announced calmly that she had news for the young parents, who were apparently cradling me in their arms, watching as I seemed to turn more blue by the minute. "Wilton is going to be all right," she said.

The miracle was not so much that I survived, but that our family came to believe that in this marvelous matriarch was a woman who had the very ear of God. For as long as she lived, until Alzheimer's disease took her from us too soon, in times of personal crisis we always felt that if we could get word of our needs to Mama Browning, she could take a request directly to God Himself. Superstitions such as the possibility that the ax could have cut Mother's pain notwithstanding, she was a woman of great faith, and she made believers of most of us.

In the coming months, the growing young family would move once again into a Glenwood Mill duplex on Blue Ridge Street, a bit more than a block from the humming manufacturing plant. Just beyond the shared center wall of the double shotgun house was another young family, that of Mr. and Mrs. Arthur Winchester. If the four adults living in the duplex had not been so busy working in the nearby mill and watching their families grow, that these two particular families wound up in the same house might have been comical. In the growing world of firearms, it might have been considered an explosive pairing - Browning and Winchester. But if the two young couples saw the irony, it was never an issue and there developed a friendship that endured for years.

And it would be in that house that in 1939 the Browning family grew yet again when in mid-August Marlene was born. This time, the days leading up to the event had gone more gently for Mother, and the ax was kept in its place in the wood crib behind the house on Turner Street. But the event itself was not without complications.

At Mother's urging and with no phones available, Dad made a hurried walk to town and to the home of Dr. Cutchens to let him know that Mother was close to delivery. There, Dad discovered that Dr. Cutchens was in Liberty, more than six miles away, called there because of some other medical emergency. His wife suggested that another Easley doctor be summoned and directed my father to that residence yet another mile away.

Dad made the walk almost at a run and there he found a physician who smelled of strong drink. Still, Dad explained the situation and the doctor promised to come as soon as he could. Dad hurried almost four miles back to the bedside of his wife. True to his word, the drunken doctor arrived soon after Dad had returned home. Though in the pain of labor, Mother was alarmed at the condition of the man who apparently was to attend this birth. Despite slurred assurances from the physician, both Mother and Dad were concerned about the child that soon was to arrive.

Then came a knocking at the door and Dad hurried to answer. There stood Dr. Cutchens.

"I'm sorry to be late," he apologized. "Just got back from a little problem in Liberty."

"We're just glad to see you," Dad said, then ushered the family physician to the room were Mother was preparing for delivery. Dr. Cutchens quickly checked Mother's condition, then pointedly pulled his fellow physician aside, lectured him concerning his inebriated condition, and sent him away.

# Come Quittin' Time

The bedside crisis had passed, and soon Marlene announced her own arrival.

Between my birth and that of Marlene, Mother and her family suffered yet another tragedy.

Like Mother, William, the youngest of the Chappell children, had spent little time in pursuing a formal education. As with hundreds of children in the first part of the 20th century, William stayed home to help with the work of sharecropping.

Tobacco was no stranger to the Chappell family, despite the poverty that was always with them. Our grandfather had what seemed permanent stains at the corners of his mouth from his chewing tobacco that seemed always to be present. He said a plug of chewing tobacco made life, in which the most common view for him was the south end of a northbound mule, a bit more bearable.

Early in his life, certainly by the age of 8, William also developed a taste for the golden leaf, but preferred his tobacco in a pouch from which he would pour and roll his own cigarettes. By the time he was 10, William was a chain smoker and no family pressure was brought to bear in opposition to his habit.

By the time he was a teenager, William also had developed asthma, perhaps driven by the tobacco-weakened condition of his young lungs. In mid-August 1937, only two months after my birth, William joined his father in putting up hay for the few farm animals available to them. He worked behind a two-mule team wagon in gathering the dried grass and tossing it into the bed of the wagon, creating a cloud of dry grass dust as he and his father worked in oppressive heat.

William began coughing. By nightfall, the coughing was almost uncontrollable. Within a day, fever gripped his frail body. When a doctor finally came to examine the 16-year-old farm boy, he discovered that William was suffering from pneumonia, for which there was at the time almost no known antidote.

He died on August 28, 1937, and was buried in a grave, near that of his sister Lula, in the cemetery at Blackjack Baptist Church.

# Chapter Five

## *'So, Where is Pearl Harbor?'*

The deaths of Mother's two younger siblings, Lula and William, had been stunning. Yet Mother found herself emotionally between her worlds of profound sadness and unbridled joy. Her baby, Marlene, was off to a good start. And, though only a few months more than two years old, I had discovered how marvelous Mama Browning's made-from-scratch biscuits were.

The sense of family and the sense of loss Mother must have felt in the deaths of Lula and William had touched neither me nor Marlene; we were too young to understand the concept of dying, and neither of us had known our departed aunt and uncle.

There were other developments on a far broader expanse that also affected our parents and, in turn, the two of us. Though Mother and Dad no longer fell under that umbrella, child labor laws finally had been enacted. In the process, the new law made our parents' the only generation in the history of the cotton industry in the South to have faced virtually a lifetime of toil in the mills.

But a new law called the Fair Labor Standards Act of 1938 had, for the first time, signaled the end of labor of children, especially in factories and mines. It also brought minimum wage rules to the work place for the first time. It mandated that Mother and Dad be paid no less than 25 cents for each hour of work, and established the work week at 44 hours, which would be amended downward in years to come. Under the new law, the minimum wage would increase to 30 cents an hour in the second year of the legislation, 1939, and to 40 cents over the following six years.

For Mother and Dad and their young family, it was welcome news not only financially, but it meant that neither Marlene nor I could be exploited as children as had our parents and hundreds of thousands of their contemporaries. At its height, it is likely, according to scholars, that more than two million children, remarkably some as young as 4, worked in factories, mines and sweat shops early in the 20th century. The U.S. Census Bureau estimated early in the 1900s that more than 18 percent of all children in the country were at work. Ours, thus, would be the first generation guaranteed a reasonably carefree childhood as a matter of law. It was a law that also had the practical effect of mandating a reasonably broad basic education. Even without the law, the reliance upon child labor in cotton mills had diminished considerably by the time of the Great Depression, thanks to random state laws that had been enacted, and to public pressure, which came mostly from what would become known as the political left. In addition, many social workers of the time became activists in calling attention to the plight of working children, and crusading newspapers, such as the *Atlanta Journal*, served to keep the practice in the public consciousness. In reality, though, aspects of the new law that established minimum wage standards in companies that employed more than a few people, and that created a uniform work week, had more far-reaching effect.

The new law made no one instantly wealthy. But the programmed minimum wage increases contained in the original version of the Fair Labor Standards Act brought hope for the future to couples such as our parents. For perhaps the first time, a whole class of workers at the bottom end of the economic scale could dream dreams of living better lives. And the act certainly offered underpinning to a growing practice of buying on credit so that firms such as Sears, Roebuck & Company became the retailer of choice for thousands of mill hill families. Almost as many homes on the mill hill treasured current issues of the Sears, Roebuck catalog as owned Bibles. And many studied the slick pages of the "wish book," as Mother called it, more religiously than they studied scripture.

The establishment of wage and hour guidelines would allow couples to compartmentalize their purchases into two categories, necessities and luxuries. Like most of the people at Glenwood Mill, Mother and Dad made a floor model Philco upright radio one of their first luxury purchases. And it probably was bought on credit.

It was an acquisition unlike any other, because it opened to us all a world of imagination.

Though radio, offering a wide choice of programming from Sunday morning gospel quartet music to farm reports, was not new at the time of their marriage, for Mother and Dad and their growing family, it still was a marvelous thing. It brought news from distant places in a reasonably timely manner. In the years ahead, it also would bring timely reports of major world events to our living room, among them baseball's World Series and presidential addresses. Even this late in my life, when I think about the World Series, then played a long way from home and in daylight, one of my first memories is a commercial jingle used for years by the company that sponsored the Series radio broadcasts.

*To look sharp ... ding! ... every time you shave,*
*To feel sharp ... ding! ... and be on the ball,*
*Just be sharp ... and skim whiskers off*
*With the modern Gillette Super Speed ...*

Mostly, though, the Philco's greatest value was that it brought escape from the tedium of the day as families gathered around to listen and to laugh.

For some time, Dad's father had been a faithful listener to the national radio comedy show, "Amos 'n' Andy." And in the early years of Mother's and Dad's marriage, we tuned in regularly to the doings of "Fibber McGee and Molly" and "The Great Gildersleeve." Via radio, we could understand even the timing of the remark when Jack Benny paused and then indignantly said with a huff, "...Well!"

Women especially were attracted to some of the radio soap operas that were aired five days a week, including "Portia Faces Life" and "The Guiding Light." The soaps were so successful that by the early 1950s, the first made-for-television daytime drama, "The First Hundred Years," hit the air. It lasted just two. In fact, television versions of our old standbys would often prove to be disappointing. Drawn from the ultra popular newspaper comic, a "Blondie" series never came close to enjoying the popularity of the newspaper panel, in part because the television family of Bumsteads suffered by comparison to that of the comic strip.

In retrospect, we know now that the comedies and the daytime dramas of 1930s and 1940s radio were far grander, in some respects, than later television versions because they were restricted only by the limits of our own imaginations. And in years to come, my own imagination seemed to have no bounds when it came to "The Lone Ranger." I still am stirred by the memory of the grand, resonant voice on the radio telling me as the show came on the air daily that *"...From out of the past come the thundering hoof beats of the great horse, Silver...."* Even the way the announcer said Silver - "SILL-vuh" - seemed magical. That introduction started low and built to a crescendo. I even enrolled in the Merita Safety Club, as Clayton Moore, the radio voice of the Lone Ranger, recommended. For a time I carried my membership card wherever I went, and I was a teenager before I discovered that Italian composer Gioachino Rossini actually had not stolen the theme music from "The Lone Ranger" in creating his "William Tell Overture." Grudgingly, I had to accept the reality that - sorry, Kimosabi - it probably happened the other way around.

Though a new medium, television, was making its first snowy appearance in the homes of common mill folk by the early 1950s, it was radio that still transported me away to the stirring music of the Cities Service Band of America.

To my ear, baseball still is best played on radio. And the first Clemson-South Carolina Big Thursday football game I ever *saw* was one carried long ago on that upright Philco.

So, despite unsettling news from Europe as the 1930s drew to a close, life held the promise of better times for Mother and Dad, though the work in the mill was getting no easier now a decade after the arrival of the Great Depression. Indeed, slasher room work continued to be physically draining for Dad, for whom sweltering heat was far more unbearable than numbing cold.

In an effort to escape the cauldron that was the slasher room long before air conditioning and humidity controls came to cotton mills, Dad had asked more than once to be moved to another section of the mill. Again and again, his requests were ignored. He would emerge daily from his shift far more haggard appearing than when he had arrived. Summertime was especially difficult. Not only did he have difficulty enduring the hot, steamy working conditions, the sultry nights robbed him of healing sleep. He always slept close to an open window, anxious for even a whisper of a cooling breeze. Too often, none came. Though still young, Dad wondered how long he would be able to endure the oppressive heat.

Easley at the time had four well-established cotton mills. Though for most of his life, Glenwood had been his home, Dad began to explore possibilities at Easley Mill, Arial and Alice, the latter the two McKissick plants.

Late in 1939, with Marlene still a babe in arms, word came that a job in the weave room at Easley Mill was his for the taking and that a house on the mill village's Third Street would be made available for the Browning family. Further, there also would be a job for Mother, though both would have to work on the first shift, from 7 a.m. until 3 p.m., which created a child care problem.

Still, Dad quickly accepted the offer and the four of us moved into the house at 708 South Third Street. It was a five-room shotgun home, the likes of which were so named because they were built to a simple plan so that, theoretically, one could open the front and back doors and fire a shotgun through the house without touching anything inside.

My aunt Virginia, the only sister among my father's six siblings, helped solve the child care problem; she became our babysitter. Turns out, I was her biggest problem and her nightmare.

By the age of 3, I was known along Third Street for my advanced skill at cussing, a talent picked up, I assume, from some of the older boys in our neighborhood. Words such as those that had found their way into my otherwise limited vocabulary certainly were never uttered in our house and never with Mother or Dad within hearing. As I recall, I was proud of my ability to sprinkle such words into my conversations even though I had no idea what some of the words meant.

Virginia tried on more than one occasion to scrub the foulness from my mouth by using soap. But my reputation in the neighborhood was at stake and, under those circumstances, one could occasionally put up with the taste of Octagon.

I did, however, try to be discrete in my use of the salty language, but it was Virginia who happened to overhear one particular speech I had for a cluster of neighborhood girls into whom I had just ridden my tricycle. She reported the nature of my comments to my father who, while normally long-abiding and compassionate, also was not known for sparing the rod.

Indeed, he spared it not at all in discussing my choice of nouns and adjectives. It was a spanking so memorable it almost drove me to cussing in front of Dad himself. I survived the corporal punishment, but not without protest.

What I did was, I ran away from home.

I decided I would move back to my Mama Browning's house at Glenwood Mill. Not that she would put up with the cussing any more than Dad would. Still, I felt it was time for me to move on, apparently. I chose a cool day to relocate and when Mother and Dad left for work at Easley Mill and Virginia sent me outside to play, I seized the opportunity. I walked down Third Street and turned right onto Seventh Avenue. At the intersection with Pendleton Street, I turned left and walked along the sidewalk past the high school and on toward town. I turned right onto East First Avenue just across the street from where the Winn-Dixie would one day be built.

In retrospect, it must have been just about here that Virginia discovered that I was missing from the neighborhood. In a panic, she sent word to Mother and Dad at the mill that I apparently had wandered away, which was not the case at all; I knew exactly where I was going and how to get there.

Alarmed, Mother and Dad hurried home from the mill to join the search.

I continued along East First Avenue, which runs in front of a building that once was the high school in Easley, past houses on the right and left that were much larger than ours on Third Street, and finally to a fork in the road where East First Avenue merges into East Main Street, then a part of busy U.S. 123 connecting Greenville and Atlanta with dozens of stops in between.

I crossed the busy highway, but other dangers lay ahead including the necessity of traversing the double tracks of the busy Southern Railway line and then crossing a narrow footpath that dissected the pond behind Glenwood Mill. I never made it that far.

As I walked along the East Main Street sidewalk opposite the armory, I came upon a place where power company crews were installing a new pole to carry the weight of the power lines. A deep hole, larger around than I, already had been dug. It was at that point that I discovered that all the walking had made me warm. I removed the thin jacket Virginia had insisted that I wear and tossed it to the bottom of the deep hole.

Two doors further along the sidewalk, I stopped to talk with two attractive older girls, Carolyn and Marjorie Merritt. They would become a part of the small-world syndrome a few years later when I became friends with their younger brother, Bill. For the moment, though, they were curious where a traveler as young as I was going.

"I'm moving back to Glenwood," I told them.

"Well, where are you moving from?" one asked.

"Easley Mill. Don't like it there."

Soon after I told them my name, one of the Merritt sisters disappeared into the house while the other suggested I stay there and rest for a few minutes, which seemed a reasonable idea to me.

Within what seemed only a few minutes, a police car, apparently summoned by the Merritts, drew up at the curb and the officer got out and joined in the conversation which, at the time, seemed not very significant to me.

"Where do you live, sonny?" he asked.

"I used to live at Easley Mill," I told him. "But I'm moving back to Glenwood. I'll live with Mama and Papa Browning when I get there."

"Why'd you decide to move?" the policeman pressed.

"'Cause I don't like it at Easley Mill."

It was remarkable, he said, that a boy no bigger than I had come so far and he wondered if I knew which streets I had walked along in getting more than halfway to the Browning home on Turner Street at Glenwood.

"Sure, I do," I said, falling for the ruse.

"You ever ridden in a police car?" he asked cheerfully.

"No, sir," I said, excited by the prospect.

"Do you want to?"

"Yes, sir."

"Tell you what, Wilton. Just for fun, let's see if you can tell me how to get back to your house at Easley Mill. Bet you can't do it."

"Bet I can," I said, accepting the challenge.

Riding shotgun in the police car, I directed the officer over a route that retraced the steps I had taken. Within a few minutes, we were riding down Pendleton Street once again, turning right onto Seventh Avenue at Easley Mill, and then turning left onto Third Street. With each turn I directed the policeman, he seemed more and more impressed so that I wondered if he could have done it without me. From my seat beside the police officer, I could see the people gathered in the distance. "I'll bet they never rode in a police car," I said to the officer.

"Some of them have," he assured me.

As we approached the house from which I intended to move, everyone's attention turned to the police car. I thought everyone was looking at me in jealousy, which turned out not to be the case.

I got more hugs in a day than I could ever remember, but Dad's mood was somber when the two of us went into a bedroom and he closed the door. He wasn't going to spank me this time, Dad announced, but he wanted to talk to me about how important I was to the family and that I should not plan on moving again. He also stressed the necessity of making sure Virginia knew my whereabouts while he and Mother were working.

"You ever take a ride in a police car?" I asked my father.

"No, son. Maybe I will some day," he said though his response, it seemed to me, lacked enthusiasm.

By the summer of 1941, a newer four-room house at the end of the street became available when the Boggs family, including my friend Gary, moved to Greenville. It was similar to other houses in the neighborhood that had been added on vacant lots at the ends of streets at Easley Mill. Unlike most of those in the community, it was not a shotgun house and it had been built beneath what already was a mature oak tree. In autumns to come, we would listen to acorns bouncing off the roof in the room nearest to the old oak, a room Marlene and I shared in those first months in our new home. Though the streets would change and become connected in years to come, it was at the time the place Third Street ended. A large pasture owned by the mill and covering perhaps 30 acres or more began at the edge of our yard, and a gate at the end of the street gave neighbors access to the grazing land for cows, kept mostly to provide milk.

Looking north from that end of the street, a pretty white church was framed almost perfectly, not far from the mill itself and at the other end of Third Street. It was the home of the

Wesleyan Methodists and, since we then owned no automobile, it was the place where we worshipped for a time.

What none of us knew at the time, of course, was this was the house that would be our family home for more than 60 years. The young, growing Browning family was home. It was there that I would grow to love living at Easley Mill and the urge to move in with my grandparents at Glenwood never came again.

It was there that the cadence of our lives was established, and it was there that some of the major events of our time reached us as reports in the newspaper and announcements on the upright Philco.

It was there that much of my own lifetime memories were born. Though I vaguely remember the day I decided to leave home in favor of my grandmother's house, the events of December 7, 1941, still are clear.

In late afternoon that day, we had gathered around the upright Philco to listen to reports of an attack on the United States Navy. Only 4 at the time, I did not fully appreciate the ramifications of the event, but Mother and Dad seemed more worried than I had ever known them to be.

The reports still were coming in that evening as Mother sifted Red Band self-rising flour and prepared to bake biscuits for our evening meal, which we called supper. There were heavy casualties, the resonant voice on the radio was telling us, and the fleet at Pearl Harbor lay in a shambles.

"So, where is Pearl Harbor?" I asked my father. "Is it anywhere close to here? And can the Japs come here?"

"It's a long way from here," he said, seeking to calm my fears. "The Japs won't be coming to drop bombs on Easley, son. I promise."

Though young, I already knew that Dad did not make promises he did not intend to keep. I felt my fears diminish.

# Chapter Six

## *The Postman's Whistle*

More than any war in which the United States had participated, World War II found its way into the homes of the American masses on a daily basis. Morning newspapers were an important part of our lives, and radio reports kept our family reasonably well informed. For children who had never been out of Pickens County - except for the time Mr. McNeely took me along on a trip to "Big Greenville" 13 miles away - Marlene and I quickly learned the names of far-away places. Before we knew for sure where Detroit was, we knew that somewhere on the other side of an ocean were places called Dunkirk, Omaha Beach, Polesti, North Africa, Monte Cassino, Stalingrad and Berlin. And places called Guadalcanal, Midway and Bataan. Several brightly colored accent pillows with such names on them adorned the sofa in our grandmother's living room, a room mostly off limits to children.

Far-away places such as those became personally important to us because three of Dad's brothers, J.C., Jack and Clarence, had gone marching off to the war. And when either

Marlene or I was invited to spend the night at Mama and Papa Browning's house, we could hear Mama praying for her soldier sons softly, fervently late into the night. It was one of the powerful ways she fought the war.

In the front room window of her house on Turner Street at Glenwood Mill was a Mother's Flag bearing three stars. Her and our grandfather's contributions to the war effort, thus, were considerable. Few families had more sons engaged in the conflict.

At home, we had our own war plans. There were scrap metal drives, and once we reached school age, we would participate in bond drives by pushing dimes into slotted cards until there were enough dimes to buy a war bond. Rationing of various kinds was imposed upon the country so that J.C., Jack and Clarence could be better supplied and equipped to fight the war, and not many people complained, least of all those of us in the Browning household. For Marlene and me, as for our parents, rationing seemed hardly inconvenient. Gasoline and rubber for automobile parts, including tires, was in short supply, but we had no automobile. Nylon stockings were relatively new in the marketplace when World War II arrived, and now the material was being used in war production, including the manufacture of parachutes. We took comfort in the hope that a strip of nylon that Mother might ordinarily have been wearing was perhaps helping Jack float safely to the earth somewhere in Europe. All in all, they seemed to be sacrifices for good and, for us, personal reasons.

Sugar was in short supply, which perhaps more directly affected Marlene and me, but Mother's cooking made up for that in dozens of ways. And Mother wanted a real bathtub, something she had never had in her life. But the metal the manufacturing of tubs would require was going into the construction of tanks and landing craft and airplanes. The bathtub would have to wait, and we would continue to bathe in the big galvanized tin washtub placed on the kitchen floor behind the wood stove and filled with steaming water heated on the spot. With wood burning in the cook stove, it was a cozy place for a bath, anyway. We also understood that J.C., Jack and Clarence might not have a bath for days as they slogged across Europe and the islands of the Pacific, so we could delay that luxury in our lives as well. Besides, nobody on the mill hill, except perhaps for those living in the super's house, had honest-to-goodness store-bought bathtubs. For years, there had seemed little need for such luxury; the mill provided bath houses with hot running water for both men and women.

There was one concession to the belt-tightening and the rationing of goods in the Browning household. Though he kept it to himself for years, Dad finally acknowledged, when it no longer mattered, that he had purchased Mother's kitchen stove on the black market, that somewhat clandestine commerce network that managed to operate outside of the country's rationing system.

We "participated" in the war in other ways, as well. There were those dark nights when "blackouts" were staged, just to make sure that the light at our window did not lead some German of Japanese bomber in our direction in the event the war in Europe or the Pacific had gone badly for the Allies, and the fighting literally turned into a world-wide war. There was something unsettling about the exercise, but it also was like a game for the two of us preschoolers as we sat there, each trying to out-quiet the other.

There also were young adults we were accustomed to seeing along Second, Third and Fourth Streets at Easley Mill who no longer were there. The Dunns, for example, had sent a son or two away to fight the Germans or the Japanese, as had Mama and Papa Browning. Occasionally, one of the fighting men would come home for a few days of furlough and they would walk proudly about the mill hill in their dress military uniforms, visiting neighbors, and calling on the parents of other military men now a long way from home. They were handsome people in their uniforms and they made us proud.

Most but not all of them made it home again, and we were reminded of that possibility on a daily basis. *The Greenville News*, as was the case with other regional newspapers, carried stories and sometimes pictures of men from Upstate South Carolina who had been listed as killed or missing in action. Even those reminders involved people we did not know, until the day the newspaper carried on its front page the picture of a handsome young man which accompanied a short story beneath the headline that read:

**Easley Man**
**Killed In Action**

He was the son of Preacher Watkins, who had been among the first fulltime pastors at Mama Browning's church, the church we would attend eventually. So, we did not actually know the young man, but we knew someone who did, and that made the death seem very close to home.

For most of the war, our lives were not remarkably different than they would have been had there been no Japanese attack on Pearl Harbor and had the German war machine not been grinding its way through neighboring countries in Europe. I was four years old - going on 10 - when the war began and Marlene was two, and young fathers with families were for a time, at least, not high on the list for the draft.

By the time I entered the first grade at West End Elementary, in the fall of 1943, I knew that these where not normal times for our country, though I had little life experience with which to compare what it meant for the United States to be at war, as opposed to at peace. But there were moments of happiness in the face of the national emergency. Jack, Clarence and J.C. had been home, at least briefly, and J.C. even had left behind a 1940 Chevrolet and had asked Dad to drive it from time to time. Jack arrived with a 1939 Plymouth and took us all for a ride around town. It was a marvelous experience.

Not as marvelous, however, as the events of March 1944. Winter had just turned to spring and when I awakened on a cool morning, I discovered that our family had grown by one. A baby daughter had been born during the night and if I would be gentle, Aunt Virginia told me, it would be all right to visit her and Mother briefly before going to school.

Mother pulled the corner of the baby's blanket back only slightly as I drew close and there was a glowing smile on Mother's face.

"This is your new sister," she said softly.

"What's her name?" I asked.

"Doris," she said. "Doris Ann Browning."

I reported the good news to my first grade teacher, Miss Carolyn Smith, when I arrived at West End. Miss Smith seemed elderly to me, with silvery gray hair, yet she seemed beautiful as well. She always smiled, and she spoke softly, never harshly as we could hear the other first grade teacher, Miss Todd, doing across the hall.

"That's wonderful news," Miss Smith said.

"OK, children," she said to the class. "Get out your pencils and paper. We will begin with our printing lesson today. I want you to write this on your papers."

She went to the blackboard and using lines that seemed to match those printed on our paper neatly placed the writing assignment on the board.

Wilton has a sister.
She is a baby sister.
Her name is Doris.

I wrote it again and again. And I memorized it.

Even though the nation was at war, the first half of the 1940s were years of considerable contentment for the young Browning family. Mother still worried about the welfare of her parents who were still living in sharecropper shacks, yet her attention to her own family was unfailing.

And like most of the fathers supporting families on the mill hill, Dad was still home with us as was Alvoid Galloway with his family next door. Mr. Nix, the postman, still made his cheerful rounds along the streets of our mill village and each time he placed an arriving letter in a mailbox, he gave his whistle two - never one, never three, but two - quick blasts to let folks know that a letter had arrived. Because of the reports from his whistle as he made his rounds, we could judge how long it would be before the postman arrived at our door.

His routine at our house most days was slightly different. On pleasant days, Mother would spend the late morning and early afternoon sitting on the back steps while Marlene and I played nearby. Then more than a year old, Doris was a growing toddler and on pleasant days would practice her new skill of walking, though uncertainly, under Mother's watchful eyes. On most days, Mr. Nix delivered the mail to Mother there, stopping as he did to visit for a moment, to remark upon how quickly we seemed to be growing. Then he would be gone, walking between Aunt Nan's and Bess White's house to begin his deliveries along Second Street. We would listen to the tweet-tweet of his whistle until we could hear it no more.

If the daily rounds by Mr. Nix helped establish an orderliness about our lives, so did Mother's daily routine. Soon after my hasty decision to move back to my grandmother's home at Glenwood Mill, Mother and Dad finally were able to arrange their own work schedules so that one or the other would be home with us all the time. Dad worked the first shift, from 7 in the morning to 3 in the afternoon, and Mother worked the second from 3 in the afternoon until 11 at night.

Though Marlene and I were in bed and sound asleep by that time, Dad always waited for Mother's arrival home shortly after 11 each night. He would stand at the top of the hill beyond our front gate and watch in the distance. He would follow Mother's walk home as she appeared in the glow of streetlights, then alternately seemed to disappear for a moment in the darkness between lights. It was a time and a neighborhood in which walking at night seemed no real threat. When Mother finally arrived at home, the two would walk into our house together, hand in hand, glad to once again be reunited.

That work schedule made for a neat division of household duties as well. Mother arose each morning in time to prepare breakfast of fried bread, jellies and coffee for Dad before he went off to the mill. For much of the rest of the morning, she did her sewing, creating aprons that were much in demand by other women working in the mill. Mother's were considered the best aprons available because the large pockets just below the waistband in front withstood the scratching and clawing of various mill tools, especially stand hooks, better than the pockets of aprons made by others. Mother's secret, she once confided, was that she always doubled the thickness of the material used to make the pockets for greater longevity.

Once she had spent time with the three of us in the backyard and collected the mail from Mr. Nix, Mother would begin preparing for her own shift in the mill by planning our dinner for the evening. It was not unusual for a pot of pinto beans to simmer on the stove in the kitchen most of the day, and Mother always prepared the dough for cornbread, poured it into a baking pan and placed it in the refrigerator with a cover of waxed paper. Dad had only to turn on the heat, remove the waxed paper, pop the pan of cornbread mix into the oven and wait. Remarkably, none of us ever tired of pinto beans and cornbread.

It thus fell Dad's lot as well to oversee school home work assignments.

Somehow, Mother also found time to tighten the large quilting frame into place in the bedroom she shared with Dad. There, stitching by hand, she created dozens of spectacular quilts of blue ribbon quality. She sold very few, instead presenting them as marvelous gifts to friends and family. When she wasn't creating spectacular hand-sewn quilts, she was busy making various afghans and throws with flying crochet needles.

She also made almost all of Marlene's and Doris' clothes through childhood and into early adulthood and beyond, and starched and ironed most of the clothing all five of us wore.

In those years, Sundays truly were days of rest and children were permitted to play, but quietly. Still, Mother had to work in her day of rest around after-church dinners that usually included cubed steak or fried chicken, hot biscuits, home-grown vegetables, and deserts, including her famous homemade coconut cakes, if we were lucky. And through it all, there were the books Mother read and treasured with deep respect. So sacred to her was the printed word that she taught the three of us to care for books in a manner that would have impressed even the authors. For example, we were not permitted to write in the margins of even our school books, dog-eared edges were to be avoided at all cost, and to fold a book until the spine would break was considered virtually unforgivable.

The three of us could not have understood the issue at the time, but it must have been this period of her marriage that underscored the likelihood that Mother would never emulate her own parents when it came to raising the three of us.

Having taught herself to read, Mother had become a voracious reader by the time the three of us arrived in the family. Though Mother for her entire life was ill at ease in the presence of school teachers, she obviously had given herself an education far more valuable, in its own way, than most of the rest of us could ever earn. And the three of us were the beneficiaries.

How else could one explain what happened to me when, as a young preschooler, I stood on a chilly early spring day looking from the window of our living room? It was the window that one day would be converted into a doorway that would connect a new wing on our house that Mother and Dad themselves would design. I watched as a lone robin red-breast pecked at the thawing ground beneath a mimosa tree that grew in our side yard. I was not aware for a time that Mother too was watching over my shoulder. Then came her soft, gentle voice, almost in a whisper reciting a four-line poem, one of hundreds, it turned out, locked joyously into her memory:

> I saw a little birdie come hop, hop, hop
> Up to the window and stop, stop, stop.
> I said, "Little birdie, how do you do?"
> He shook his little tail and away he flew.

The robin looked toward the window and seemed to have heard. He shook his tail and flew away. The bird's timing and the smile on Mother's face was perfect as she embraced me.

It is sad now to consider the possibility that she knew no moments such as that when she was a child. There must have been little time for that sort of joyousness when, certainly by the age of 8, she was forced to shoulder the burden of being the bread-winning lady of the house.

There was little beyond the war itself to intrude upon this seemingly idyllic world in which the three of us little Brownings were thriving. We had no automobile, except those on loan from our uncles, J.C. and Jack and, later, a burgundy-colored Chevrolet coupe Clarence bought and pampered and which I thought, and still think, might have been the most beautiful

car in the world. But the Wesleyan Methodist Church was only the distance of Third Street from our home and for a time we regularly attended Sunday School, preaching and Vacation Bible School there.

Not even the arrival of a sweetly scented letter, that brought Mr. Nix, the postman, tweeting cheerily upon his whistle when he dropped the seemingly special message into our mailbox, could intrude in an unwelcome way into our lives. It was addressed to a Browning, but not one who lived at 712 Third Street at Easley Mill. Mr. Nix did not have to sound his whistle when he arrived at our doorstep on his rounds the next day; Mother awaited him at the front door, the unopened letter that reeked of lavender held in her hand.

"You delivered this yesterday by mistake," she said pointedly to the friendly postman. "This Browning does not live here."

"Beg pardon, Mrs. Browning," he said, apparently with a sincerity he may not have truly felt. "I understand."

For days thereafter, the wayward letter, apparently a love message, became the genesis of daily reports from Mr. Nix.

"Ahhh, Mrs. Browning," he said on one occasion. "I hope I'm not saying anything out of line, mind you. But there's a certain lady up town who just got the latest washing machine Sears sells. You ought to see it. Somebody must think an awful lot of that young woman."

He laughed and was on his way.

"Maybe you've heard," he said a few days later, "but just in case you haven't, there's a certain young woman showing up about town in a fancy new mink coat. Where do you reckon she got a thing like that?"

"Why, Mr. Nix, I would have no idea. How about you?"

"Wouldn't know, Mrs. Browning. Wouldn't know."

And so it went, through the winter of 1944-45 and into the first hints of spring. It was a playful exchange between Mother and the postman in which Mother came to willingly play along.

In April, a year after Doris' birth, Mr. Nix as usual found mother sitting on the back steps of our house at the end of Third Street. She had expected him at any minute, but still had not seen his arrival nor heard the approaching tweet-tweeting of his whistle. On this day, he walked as he always did between our house and the Galloway's. And, as usual, he carried the day's mail in his hand, a solitary envelope.

This time, there was no laughter in the postman's voice.

"Any news about the other woman?" Mother asked.

"Not today," he answered somberly. He handed Mother the single sealed envelope. The postman knew from long experience the message contained within.

"I'm sorry, Mrs. Browning," he said softly as he handed our Father's greeting from the draft board to Mother.

Her hands trembled as she took the piece of mail that had the potential of changing the lives of us all. "I am very sorry," Mr. Nix said again.

Tears rolled down Mother's cheeks and she sobbed deeply, and Mr. Nix lingered, delaying the rest of his round, figuratively giving Mother a shoulder on which to cry. He stayed for a time, speaking softly to the pretty young mother.

"Mrs. Browning, I have other mail to deliver," he finally said softly. She nodded approvingly and tried to fight back yet another wave of tears.

"Can I see if Bess White's home? Or Aunt Nan? Maybe one of them could come be with you for a while until Mr. Browning gets home from work. I'd say Ina might come, but I just delivered the same message to the Galloways for Alvoid. I guess both Mr. Browning and Mr. Galloway are being called up."

"I'll be all right," Mother said though still fighting the emotions that were tearing at her heart. "And I'll check on Ina in a bit."

"You know, Mrs. Browning, the war's been going well lately," Mr. Nix said, trying to find the silver lining. "I'll bet Mr. Browning will be back home before you know it. The Germans can't last much longer, and the war in the Pacific is moving closer and closer to Japan. Who knows? Mr. Browning might not get there in time to see any action."

"Thank you, Mr. Nix," Mother said as she could feel her emotions finally being reigned in. She knew Mr. Nix's optimism was perhaps misplaced, but she appreciated it nonetheless.

Dad had a few days to get his affairs in order before he and Alvoid were to report for induction to Fort Jackson near Columbia, South Carolina. There they were told to return home and await further word from the War Department.

"Further word" for both Dad and Alvoid came in mid-April, notifying them that they were to report for training. On the appointed day, the five of us arose earlier than usual and we sat around the table while Dad had perhaps one final home-cooked breakfast before becoming a soldier or a sailor. And we all huddled around mother for a family hug at the back door.

"Willie! You ready?" Alvoid, our neighbor, called from the yard. Dad lingered as he kissed Mother one last time, and we watched the two mill hands walk away and down the back alley toward Seventh Avenue, marching off to war.

We watched, occasionally waving, until they were out of sight. And then we watched a while longer. Finally, Mother closed the back door.

"You and Marlene go back to bed and rest a while," she suggested. "I'll get up in a bit and fix you some breakfast."

We did as we were told, except neither of us could sleep. We both were old enough to understand in an elementary way the ramifications of what had just happened. We knew there was a chance that Dad and Alvoid might never come home again, or that one perhaps would return, but not the other.

What we did not know was that the two next-door-neighbor soldiers-to-be would be home sooner than we had expected. Indeed, we still were in our sleepless beds and Mother still lingered in her bedroom with Doris tucked in with her when we heard a sound once again at the back door.

"It's Dad!" I called out. I could tell by his footsteps. Marlene and I rushed into the living room and toward the kitchen where Mother and Dad already were in an embrace for the ages.

"What happened?" Mother asked finally.

"When we got to the bus station," Dad said, "there was a sailor at the door to the bus. He was telling anyone who had been called up to go back home, that the war soon would be over and we'd be called if we were going to be needed."

The calls for Dad and Alvoid never came.

I always tell younger generations of Brownings that Dad and Alvoid were the people who won the war in Europe, that once the Germans found out they were coming, they threw down their weapons and gave up.

# Chapter Seven

## The Zip-Ah-Dee-Doo-Dah Years

If the suggestion that Dad and Alvoid were responsible for the end of the war in Europe lacked credibility, it was not debatable that they were among the first people in Easley to know that the conflict against Germany was near an end. Once the realization had settled in that Dad probably would not have to enter military service, yet another happy thought took its place in our lives:

Clarence, J.C. and Jack also soon would be coming home.

It was news that was especially sweet at the home of our grandparents on Turner Street at Glenwood Mill. Mama Browning prayed long and fervently every day for her three sons in uniform, for American sons in general, and for the eventual defeat of the Axis powers. Still, three times during the war, Western Union telegrams had arrived at Mama and Papa Browning's door. All three times, Mama placed the unopened message on the kitchen table and hurried off to her bedroom to pray yet again. Whatever sad news was contained in each of those three yellow envelopes, however it might change the lives of all of us, was in the Lord's hands, she always prayed on those occasions. And each of us also was in His hands. She sought the grace and strength to deal with the news, whatever it may be, that lay unopened on her enameled kitchen table.

Each of the three times she emerged from her prayers for her sons, she returned to the kitchen table and, with trembling hands, opened the telegrams. Each of the three brought word that one of her sons had been wounded in action. J.C. would wind up with a Purple Heart, Jack with a Purple Heart with Oak Leaf Cluster.

Despite the wounds, all three sons would make it safely home again, and the Mother's Flag with its three gold stars would come down from its place of honor in the front room window, folded neatly and put away for the ages.

And when victory in Europe was finally declared, the whistle at Easley Mill began wailing and mill hands who owned cars rushed to their machines and began blowing their horns. People who lived on the mill hill hurried into the streets for the celebration that lasted into the evening. People who perhaps had not spoken in months or years embraced.

It was over. Could the fall of the Japanese be far behind? It seemed even more remote that Dad and Alvoid would ever have to go marching off to war.

Like many Americans, including a large percentage of those living on mill hills in the South, Mother and Dad had cultivated a small Victory Garden in a corner of the backyard during the war years. It was a plot of land that in the years just after the war Dad converted, perhaps appropriately, to a peaceful flower garden. There he grew a variety of dahlias, some with single blooms as large as dinner plates, others with centers of playful curly petals and still others that bloomed into large balls of rich color. They were cut frequently and were placed about our house, taken to the homes of sick friends and neighbors and hauled off to church early on Sunday morning to be placed as the centerpiece at the altar. By the second year of the garden, the dahlias were joined by gladiolas that became the beautifully fanned backdrop for the dahlias in the flower arrangements that found their way to church and about the neighborhood.

His flowers also had attracted the attention of Mrs. Lois McCauley, who ran a flower shop in Easley, as she was making a delivery one early summer day near the end of Third Street. It was Mrs. McCauley, then known as Easley's "flower lady," who suggested adding gladiolas to the garden and for more than three years, Dad supplied Mrs. McCauley with fresh dahlias and gladiolas for her shop.

But the dahlias became a matter of the most pride for Dad and on perfect days, which seemed to come more frequently during times of peace, he would hoist Doris upon his broad shoulders and the two of them would walk among the array of flowering plants with Dad singing to his beloved child, and perhaps to his beloved flowers as well, from "Song of the South":

> *Zip-a-dee-doo-dah,*
> *Zip-ah-dee-ay.*
> *My, oh my, what a wonderful day!*
> *Plenty of sunshine, headin' my way.*
> *Zip-a-dee-doo-dah,*
> *Zip-ah-dee-ay.*
>
> *Mister Bluebird's on my shoulder.*
> *It's the truth, it's actual,*
> *Everything is satisfactual.*
> *Zip-a-dee-doo-dah,*
> *Zip-ah-dee-ay.*
> *Wonderful feeling, wonderful day.*

Doris' joyous laugh, beautiful and exciting, became the accompanying music for Dad's solos. In a real sense, we were living in a zip-a-dee-doo-dah world, even if we were reminded from time to time in a shocking way that ours was not always a perfect world.

Close to a decade earlier when Mother and Dad were first married and rented their first mill house, the rent rate was 25 cents a room per month and included water, sewer and electricity. In some mill villages in the South, though not at either Glenwood Mill or Easley Mill, the rent also included basic and unpretentious furniture, such as kitchen tables, chairs and stoves and perhaps a couple of creaking bed frames.

By the early post-war years, the rent had increased, but not dramatically, and still included utilities, which created a bit of a problem at our house. Since rent included electrical power, there were no individual meters on the homes. Instead, the houses on an entire street were rigged as one continuous circuit. With each house in a sense considered a separate room, it was, as in the case of Third Street on which we lived, like electrifying a 28-room house. And on Third Street, there was one major ground wire for the entire circuit, and it was at our house, driven into the red clay hard against one of the brick pillars that supported the structure.

It was not unusual to hear a loud cracking and feel the house shutter when lightning struck anywhere along Third Street as the powerful bolt was carried harmlessly, if frighteningly, away by the ground wire at our house.

Even more disconcerting was the fact that we always were the first people on the street to know that someone, perhaps the Cothrans who lived at least 300 yards away, had a short circuit in one of their few appliances. If one of us touched the Westinghouse ice box and received an electrical jolt, or Mother was mildly stunned when she plugged in her Maytag wringer washing machine, it was a signal to start making the rounds. Dad would canvass one side of the street and Mother the other and they would knock on every door along Third Street asking neighbors to check their appliances for shorted-out circuits. When the problem was finally detected and corrected, the shocking episodes at our house disappeared, until the next short circuit on Third Street.

But wiring wasn't the only problem that came with mill houses. Another had to do with what to do with the dead.

It was a time when the viewings of the deceased were normally held in the home in which they lived or in the home of a son or daughter, instead of the solons of funeral homes as is customary now. And when that viewing involved some of the mill houses, particularly those built like ours, getting the dearly departed home one last time apparently was no easy task.

When a hearse bearing the remains of the elderly grandmother of a family in the community arrived in the neighborhood one warm summer day, some of us gathered in a nearby yard to watch as the coffin apparently bearing the body of the dead woman was removed from the back of the hearse. When the mortuary workers tried to move the coffin into the house, they found that the front door was too narrow, which occasionally was the case. They had but one alternative. The windows were wider than the doors, so a couple of additional strong backs were recruited, the window sash opened to its widest, and the coffin passed from the front porch to the living room through the window.

An hour before the funeral, the body was passed back out of the house in the same manner at the start of the journey to a final resting place.

Still, when the companies decided to sell the mill houses in the early 1950s, renters were given first options on the homes in which they were living. And most of them decided to buy. On the day Dad and Mother made the commitment to own our home, Dad was a worried man, not certain he would ever be able to pay off the mortgage. The purchase price for our four-room house a staggering $3,500.

All in all, the years following the war were wonderful years, full of hope and dreams for young mill hand parents and their children who, it was widely assumed, also would become mill hands in the years to come. No one knew at the time, of course, that the booming textile industry would fall upon hard, if not fatal, times. Nor that Easley Mill itself would shut down forever in our lifetimes and become a mere shell with rogue trees trying to grow from an unlikely perch, the top rim of its tall smokestack. Though company stores no longer were in operation by the end of the war where we lived, the script system of compensation long past, and our interests were more and more being drawn beyond the boundaries of the mill hill, we still had enough drama and uncertainty in our lives.

For example, in the late 1940s, it seemed to become important to our Mother and Father, and to some degree to the three of us, whether Gravel Gerti really was interested in B.O. Plenty, or perhaps she merely was playing him along. Gravel and B.O. were people of questionable pedigree who came to our breakfast table every day in the Dick Tracy comic strip in *The Greenville News*. While Tracy himself was hunting down gangsters and talking on his two-way wrist radio there, indeed, seemed to be romance afoot, and that was enough to set Mother and Dad to daily discussing whether or not this was a good thing.

There would be a certain controlled excitement eventually about nuptials in which Gravel would become Mrs. B.O. Plenty. And subsequently, when it seemed certain that a comic strip child was likely for the Plentys, we all wondered if it would be a girl and look like Gravel, or a son and - heaven forbid! - look like B.O. And what name would be given the child?

# Come Quittin' Time

When Sparkle Plenty was born, it was a special day in the Browning household. Not as important as when Doris was born, or when Jack, J.C. and Clarence came home from the war. But important, nonetheless. So much so that when a new puppy, a feisty little mixed breed with white fur and black spots, came to live at our house, we did not debate for long about what name our new pet would have. She was named Sparkle. We wound up calling her Sparkie.

Our family was not alone in following the romance, wedding and parenthood of the Plentys. About the time Gravel was delivering Sparkle, a baby girl was being born to the Whitlocks who lived down the street in a house near the intersection of Third Street and Seventh Avenue. She was named Sharon, but from infancy she was called Sparkle, a nickname that stuck until Sharon was well into adulthood.

The interest in the Plentys and in the Dick Tracy comic strip in general at the Browning house had waned considerably by the time Sparkle, the comic strip daughter, had become a young lady and, in turn, had given birth to her own child, Sparkle Plenty Jr.

The Plenty family was growing, and the Browning family was growing up, and without knowing it, the three of us had become part of the television generation on the mill hill.

At the time of the start of World War II, most of the adults living on our mill hill were without automobiles and had little need for such since the cotton mill itself was no further than a half mile from any point in our community. But by 1950, we Brownings had become part of a more mobile community. Dad had purchased our first car, a 1940 Plymouth four-door, the car in which I learned to drive and which I twice wrecked.

The used Plymouth was just one of two marvelous developments at our house during the period. We also had a telephone for the first time, and Dad cut a hole in the plaster wall between the living room and our bedroom and installed a small pocket door and a slot where the phone book was to be placed. The phone could, therefore, be passed back and forth between the two rooms, depending upon the level of privacy one desired. In his wisdom, Dad understood that the time perhaps would come when boyfriends or a girlfriend might be on the other end of the line, and the conversations soft and not intended for general family consumption. We were assigned phone number 6066 and cheerfully shared the line with three other "parties," neighbors of ours who, we were certain, occasionally listened in on our telephone conversations.

But the Plymouth was the machine that gave us flight, in a sense.

It was a car with a stumpy knob-like mechanism just to the right and above the accelerator which was the car's starter. Though not a tall man, Dad could reach the starter without difficulty with his right foot so that his heel also depressed the accelerator encouraging just enough flow of gasoline, which sold for 19 cents a gallon, to bring the engine to life. The reach to the starter was a bit more of a challenge for me. Like almost all cars of the era, the Plymouth was powered by a manual transmission and the gear lever was just back of the steering wheel. It required a long, sweeping movement of the gear shift to progress from low to second, then back down to high. Like the starter, the dimmer switch for the headlights also was on the floor and to the left of the steering column.

We had become the owners of the Plymouth at a time when the pumps at most gasoline stations were attended. It was rare for one to step from a car to pump gasoline. "A dollar's worth" would be enough gasoline for most of the week, motorist insurance was not required and seldom bought, and in South Carolina one could obtain a license to drive at the age of only 14. The license itself was a thin sliver of metal with the name and address of the owner of the license stamped into the finish by some sort of mechanical typewriter. It looked a bit like a military dog tag and clipped handily to the key ring. It was handy for twisting small screws into place and, thus, frequently was slightly bent.

That Plymouth was a marvelous thing for the Browning family. It not only made it possible for the five of us to more easily now become active in the Easley Church of God, which Dad once had served, though very young, as the Sunday School superintendent. Perhaps as importantly, it gave Mother, who never drove, the means to more frequently look in on her own mother and father in that series of sharecropper shacks in which they continued to live, usually in Oconee County.

But it was television, perhaps more than any other single advancement, which seemed to set our imaginations to flight, though apparently not always in the most positive manner. At the invitation of my uncle Wallace, I had "seen" television a few years earlier when I accompanied him to a friend's house along Hagood Street at Glenwood Mill on New Year's Day to watch the Rose Bowl football game. "Watching" the game was an exaggeration. Though it seemed marvelous at the time to see the shadowy figure of a football player actually running at almost that very moment on a football field on the other side of the country, to say we were "watching" the game was giving more credit than the technology deserved at the time. What we watched for most of the afternoon was a glowing, unsteady field of television "snow."

A large, bulky RCA black-and-white, the only kind available, television purchased jointly by Dad and me, with my contributions coming from the proceeds of my paper route, was perhaps the first on Third Street. But the first television in our neighborhood belonged to Aunt Nan Ledford, whose yard adjoined ours at the back alley.

Aunt Nan was perfectly cast as a grandmother, which she was, with dark hair despite her advancing years. She spoke always softly, and with a gentle smile, and her closest neighbors, including us Brownings and Bess White who lived next door, were considered almost as close as relatives.

In the early 1950s, Aunt Nan still worked in the mill as did all of her adult neighbors. She also cared for her husband who long ago, we were told, returned from World War I not the same man who had gone away. He had come under the spell, they said, of the fearful mustard gas of that great conflict, became a prisoner of war and for a time was buried alive. His body, if not his spirit, survived. But in what were supposed to be the golden years of his life, he lived a mostly reclusive existence, though he could be seen puttering about the yard on rare occasions, neither greeting nor engaging neighbors in conversation.

In a younger, more vital time, he had driven a convertible home, parked it in the backyard of his and Aunt Nan's home at the end of Second Street, and never moved it again. With its fenders rusting away and the interior upholstery smelling of wind, rain and sun, it was left to the elements and to a few of us neighborhood kids. Aunt Nan never suggested that we find other amusement, and there were days when, playing alone, I would sit for hours moving the steering wheel, pretending to change gears, listening to the revving of the engine, though the only engine noise was one that came from my own imagination. I made imaginary trips driving as far and as wide as my world at the time, occasionally all the way to Mama Browning's house perhaps three miles away, and even to "Big Greenville," that destination I had shared with Mr. McNeely, though I wasn't sure I knew the way precisely. But my imagination was wonderfully forgiving of such deficiencies.

Aunt Nan would invite us in from time to time to watch whatever was being shown on the only channel her television could display with any degree of clarity, WFBC-TV, Channel 4, in Greenville.

Doris especially was a frequent guest before Aunt Nan's television, and she became enthralled even in the telecasts of the weekly fights. She missed nothing, especially the catchy jingles of products advertised on the fights and other programs she occasionally watched.

It was because of this fascination that Doris, our baby sister, the cute little bundle of joy with the long, golden Shirley Temple curls tumbling down her shoulders, came home singing the jingles she had heard on Aunt Nan's television.

*What'll you have? Pabst Blue Ribbon.*
*What'll you have? Pabst Blue Ribbon.*
*What'll you have? Pabst Blue Ribbon.*
*Pabst Blue Ribbon Beer.*

*Fresher, cleaner, smoother flavor,*
*Zest and sparkle millions favor ...*

It was at just about this point in the jingle that Mother became alarmed at Doris' choice of songs. This was no "Jesus Loves Me" that she had learned in Sunday School. No "I'll Be A Sunbeam."

This was beer, and it was being impressed upon us that beer was never to cross our lips, either as liquid or as song, though rumor had it that some of our uncles, and perhaps an aunt or two, may have tasted such.

Even though she still was of a tender age, Doris received a strong lesson regarding the evils of strong drink, including fresher, cleaner, smoother Pabst Blue Ribbon beer. It was a lecture that ended, as did all of those Mother delivered to us, with the warning, "Just wait 'til your Dad gets home."

Television, of course, would impact our lives in the years to come in ways some of us could not have imagined.

As a teenager, I earned spending money not only by delivering *The Greenville News* to customers on the mill hill, but also by working weekday afternoons and Saturdays at Pickensville Grocery. One of my early-week jobs on the day the weekly shipment of stock arrived at the loading dock at the side of the store was to set all the shipping boxes of feminine hygiene products aside. Then, one by one, I was assigned the chore of neatly wrapping in plain brown paper each individual package of sanitary napkins before placing the merchandise in its assigned shelf position in the store. Despite the manufacturers' expense in attempting to create name recognition and logos, no identifying marks could be displayed.

Such were the sensitivities of the man who operated the grocery, Hayward Harris, a good man of impeccable character and, to the extent possible in his store, the protector of our sensibilities.

In recent years, I have wondered if Hayward watched much television, the medium that now brings to our dens and living room advertisements suggesting that we speak with our doctors about a whole range of personal problems ranging from gastric distress to sexual dysfunction.

It perhaps happened long before we were aware of it, but for those of us on the mill hill, that genie escaped the bottle in the early 1950s. Television and the post-war surge in automobile ownership changed our lives forever.

By the time the glows of televisions began to show up in the living rooms of mill houses, Mama and Papa Browning had moved from Turner to Barton Street which made the walk to work at Glenwood Mill even shorter, just two blocks. And it was with some anticipation that our grandfather awaited the delivery of his first television set. When it arrived, he placed a call to 6066, our phone. Beating me to the phone, Marlene answered.

"I was just wondering if you and Wilton and Doris might like to come over and watch my new television," he said, hiding his dry humor. "You ever seen a color picture on television?"

"No, sir," Marlene responded excitedly.

"Well, I've got one."

Having thus been invited to view the first color television any of us had seen, and certainly the first in Easley, we piled into the Plymouth, all five Brownings, and headed to Glenwood and Barton Street.

"Y'all come in and have a seat," our grandfather said when we arrived. There was a sly smile on his face. "Just a minute and I'll turn it on."

When Papa moved away from the screen, there it was, color television. He had installed a series of colored cellophane sheets to the front of the new TV set.

"See," he said, delighted that his practical joke had worked, "this is what a color picture looks like when it's red," he said, pressing the red sheet against the black-and-white picture. He then moved it away. "And if you want blue, this is it." He flattened the blue sheet of cellophane across the picture. "How 'bout green? Anybody like green?" he asked, and the green sheet was placed across the picture.

We all sat stunned.

It would be years before we would finally see an honest-to-goodness color picture on television, and even longer before we would see one in which the colors did not run together in some confused pattern so that faces were often green and clouds purple.

Though beer apparently was not a part of it, Doris would develop a special affinity for the fast life, an aspect of her personality about which the rest of her family knew almost nothing until the three of us were well into adulthood.

By the time they were teenagers, Doris and Becky Sizemore, a Third Street neighbor just five doors from our home, had been friends for most of their lives and even had double dated together.

Becky had become fond of a young man named Joe Tom Crews, who liked fast cars and who introduced Doris, in Becky's company, to the outlaw Friday night drag races on a stretch of abandoned highway not far from Pickens, South Carolina. For Doris, there was a special fascination in the dangerous sport whose participants were mostly teenage boys from mill hills in Easley, Liberty and Pickens.

"I'd like to do that, just one time," Doris said over the roar of the engines as she attended one of the Friday night speed rumbles.

"You're welcome to make a run in my car," Joe Tom offered. And Doris quickly accepted the invitation. She won the first heat she ever ran, and became something of a driving sensation at the Friday night races, though no one in the immediate family was aware of her new-found talent. So quick was her move in shifting gears that other male drivers frequently asked her to make runs in their machines, just as a basis of comparison to other fast cars at the track.

Doris won again and again. But she knew how to keep a secret.

A few years later, she would keep another secret. When her boyfriend, Obie Tinsley, whom she met through Joe Tom, presented Doris with a diamond engagement ring when she was in the 8th grade, as expected the development caused great concern in our home. Would Doris complete her high school education, or would she not? Both Doris and Obie promised that the engagement would not prevent Doris from attaining her diploma, and that the wedding itself would not take place until no earlier than the summer following graduation.

With Doris wearing the white Easter dress Mother had made for her, the two were secretly married in Clarksville, Georgia, in the summer before the start of Doris' senior year. The promise made by the engaged couple to delay the wedding did not hold, but the secret of the newlyweds did. So well was the secret of their Georgia wedding kept that no one in the family learned the truth for years, and Mr. and Mrs. Tinsley were re-married in a church wedding complete with white wedding gown, maid of honor, best man, flowers and tearful mothers. It all was done for the benefit of family and friends and to sustain their secret. One of the ironies was that the second wedding was so complete that Dad walked Doris down the aisle and gave her hand to Obie. The father's role is, of course, a symbolic one. But Dad went to his grave not aware that his giving Doris in marriage was truly symbolic and nothing more.

Almost from the beginning, Obie was an abusive husband, yet another development that Doris also was successful in keeping hidden for most of 25 years. Despite the abuse, the union produced three children who were the pride of their mother and a joy to their grandparents.

But Marlene's wedding, coming in 1959, was not a merely symbolic one, and Mother's skill as an organizer was never more obvious. While such events are a year or more in the planning, Mother arranged for a church wedding in just five hours.

Marlene had dated Charles Burke, a control tower operator at Donaldson Air Force Base in Greenville, South Carolina, for several months, and the two were in love. More than once, he had asked Marlene to become his wife. Again and again, she had hesitated and now Charles would soon be departing for the start of a three-year tour of duty in Japan.

"Let's wait until you get back," Marlene suggested as the two talked quietly on a Sunday evening.

"If I go to Japan," Charles answered softly, "I won't be coming back. That wouldn't be right. In three years, you would meet someone else and there would be no reason for me to come back. Come go with me."

Marlene hesitated, her heart racing, then she said yes.

On Monday, Marlene called the church pastor, E.B. Rose, to inquire about his availability for a wedding. Tuesday evening at the church parsonage on Katherine Street in Easley would be fine, he said. The wedding was on, but it would not be the simple ceremony Marlene and Charles envisioned.

Just before Marlene left for a half day of work at Stone Manufacturing Company in Greenville on Tuesday morning, she confirmed to her still-doubting mother that she would be getting married that evening and asked if Mother could iron her dress of organza which she planned to wear for the ceremony.

Mother said she would.

But by the time Marlene returned home near 2 p.m., the plans had changed and Marlene had had no role in the changes.

The small, quiet ceremony had become a church wedding, even if there was no time for invitations to be mailed to a long list of invitees. Mother had sprung into action, first by enlisting my mother-in-law, Beulah Cantrell, to handle the reception and to do much of the decorating. Mrs. Cantrell also produced the wedding gown my wife, Joyce, had worn for our nuptials in 1956 and the lacy wedding dress was a perfect fit for Marlene. She would not be wearing organza.

Mother's next urgent call had been to Lois McCauley, Easley's "flower lady," who put less pressing work aside and rushed into the Easley Church of God in mid-afternoon and did her magic with flowers. With Mrs. McCauley and Mrs. Cantrell working together, the church looked as though this wedding had been months in the planning.

And, yes, Margaret Edgar would be available to provide the music. Doris and Betty Browning, Clarence's older daughter, would stand with Marlene. One of Charles' Air Force buddies, Jim Caine, would be at his side for the wedding as Charles' best man.

There was only left to check with Preacher Rose to make sure he understood the change in plans from his parsonage home to his church. But there was a problem, he said. It was to be the first wedding Preacher Rose had ever performed and he was not certain a marriage license obtained in Greenville County, where Donaldson Air Force Base was located, would be sufficient for a wedding taking place in Pickens County, nor that he would be allowed to preside under such circumstances.

It took calls to attorneys to persuade the parson that no laws were being broken or bent. And the wedding was on.

It was Marlene's wedding, but it also was the wedding Mother never had. When she and Dad pledged their lives to each other, two friends and Mrs. Graham, the pastor's wife, were the only witnesses. Neither his parents nor hers had attended the brief ceremony at Glenwood Mill.

A description of Marlene's church wedding was printed in the local newspaper, the *Easley Progress*, on the same page announcing the birth of our second child, Vicky, in Kansas where, like Charles, I was serving in the Air Force.

Importantly, the promise Doris was able to keep was to complete her high school education. Indeed, her graduation in early June 1962 was one of the proudest moments in our Mother's life. Though Mother always had encouraged us in our studies, she never personalized our education to her benefit. Still, when Doris graduated, Mother had seen all three of her children reach an education plateau of immense importance to her. For a woman who almost certainly never finished the second grade before going to work, the accomplishment, akin to a houseful of children receiving advanced college degrees today, left Mother almost speechless. But still she managed to point out the matter of pride to anyone who would listen. As the days following Doris' graduation faded into memory, there were fewer and fewer people willing to listen. Mother had discussed with all her co-workers and most of our neighbors in considerable detail how proud she was, and most of them had been told several times.

What we could understand, finally, was the reason behind Mother's ever-present respect for school teachers. Never timid in almost all other facets of her life, Mother held teachers in such high regard that she almost always was awed in their presence. The feeling was so deep that Mother as often as she could would avoid parent-teacher conferences, enlisting Dad as the parental representative most of the time because of her fear that she would develop a case of stammering in the presence of our teachers. Only one time did Mother ever personally call for a conference with a teacher, that coming when she felt that Marlene had not been treated well by one of her high school instructors. This time, because one of her children had, in her view, been mistreated, Mother had no difficulty speaking her mind. For days thereafter, she felt guilty because she had brought a teacher to tears.

Though lacking proper schooling herself, for Mother education was perhaps the highest calling. It was so important, in her opinion, that for one who had only barely tasted anything close to a formal schooling, Mother became one of the most educated people I have known because of her love for reading.

And somewhere along the way, she also learned the fine art of negotiation. Her most important weapon in any negotiation was her biscuits.

She was a master at the art of creating perfect biscuits. They always were fluffy, never heavy and doughy, invariably the perfect size and cooked to a golden brown, though she always returned a few to the oven to be virtually burned for Dad because that's the way he liked them best.

Mother understood that hers were biscuits that rivaled even those of Mama Browning and Mama's sister, Rosie Lee, who made tiny biscuits barely larger than a silver dollar that always were one of the hits of the Gray reunions in Hart County, Georgia. And Mother was never reluctant to play the biscuit card.

"If you'll come over and cut my grass," she would say, for example, "I'll put on some biscuits and we'll have some biscuits and gravy."

"Come by when you get a chance and put up my Christmas tree and I'll cook us a pan of biscuits and some cubed steak."

"Reckon you could drop by and drive me to the store to do a little shopping? I'll fix some biscuits and warm up the chicken we had last night."

There was nothing Mother would not try to buy with her biscuits, including her very life and that of her granddaughter, Dee.

Willie Lee Browning: Twice he tried employment outside textiles, but always came back.

Martha Chappell: Before she became a Browning she became Miss Arial, a beauty queen.

Newly-weds Ambrose and Cleo Tweeter Chappell: Their life would never be this good.

Our Grandfather Chappell: He spent a lifetime clawing a living out of red clay soil.

Papa Browning, our grandfather, with the author. He made one bad turn and never drove again.

Easley Mill is now only a shell. Small trees try to grow from the top of the tall stack.

Union Church where Mother was baptized still stands. It's an apartment building now.

Decaying Newry Mill, the place where Martha, the child, began her long textile labors.

As a child laborer, Mother used to climb high into the Newry tower for cool air, rest.

This became Mother's home away from home, a marked improvement over her family's shack.

They called him Bill when Dad drove this Model A on his first date with Mother.

Mother's brother and sister, who died young, rest near each other
at Mount Pleasant in Oconee County.

# Chapter Eight

## *Open Door Policy*

In most ways, Mother was the embodiment of mill hill values, among them a trusting nature. In my own years of growing up on the mill hill, there were never any crime waves and virtually no need for locks and locksmiths. In the days before window air conditioners hummed throughout the neighborhood, everyone slept in the summertime with windows wide open to capture any hint of a cooling breeze.

In my mid-teen years, I worked at a grocery store not far from the mill hill, and among my duties was to regularly deliver the weekly supply of food stuffs to many of the same people to whom I also delivered the morning newspaper. In many cases, I arrived with groceries at homes in which everyone was putting in their eight hours at the nearby mill, usually in the weave room or spinning room.

"Heyward," they would frequently tell my boss when calling in their orders, "I've only got a $10 bill, so be sure to send change." With the leanest grade of hamburger selling at three pounds for $1, $10 in most cases would cover a week's groceries.

In those cases, the $10 would be lying prominently on the kitchen table, perhaps weighted down by a salt shaker, where the non-perishables were to be left. It was my duty to put food that needed refrigeration - meats, milk and eggs - safely away in the refrigerator or one of the few ice boxes still around, and to leave the change for the $10 in place on the table.

Without being overly curious, we also considered it proper to quickly look about, just to make sure any beans left simmering on the stove had enough water so that they would not burn, and that everything seemed in order in the home.

It was so much an open society in that regard that someone suggested to a neighbor on Second Street that locking the doors when the tenants were away might be a good idea. After all, it had been noted in the newspaper that bad things sometimes happened in Greenville, and we were only 30 minutes away.

"Not much need locking our doors," the neighbor said, echoing Mr. Hopkins' sentiments. "All we've got for the locks are skeleton keys, and everybody on the mill hill has the same skeleton key. So, I don't reckon locking doors makes much sense."

And so the doors remained mostly unlocked, including those in our home at the end of Third Street. And for the Smiths, who lived across the street from us, that was perhaps a good thing.

"I said our house is on fire!" the familiar voice in the living room had said loudly and with appropriate urgency.

My sisters and I had awakened about the same time and squinted toward the windows in the room we shared. The darkness that enveloped us told us it was the middle of the night. But we were suddenly awake enough to hurry into the living room.

There, on the telephone just outside our bedroom door, was Richard, Frances Smith's second oldest, a handsome early teenager who stood there bare-footed and in his pajamas despite the numbing wintertime cold outside.

"711 Third Street," he was saying with alarm heavy in his voice. "End of Third Street at Easley Mill!

"Please hurry!"

And so they had, the fire trucks wailing in the distance and drawing ever closer until they were there, one with its lights flashing backing into the Smith's driveway, the other blocking the end of Third Street. Firemen rushed in to discover a chimney fire which had sent scorching fingers of flame into a nearby closet.

It could have been worse, much worse, the fire captain was telling Mrs. Smith, had Richard not acted so quickly. So quickly, indeed, that he had hurried to what he knew was the nearest phone, the one in our living room. And he had simply opened the unlocked front door, turned on a light and had dialed the number for the Easley Fire Department.

It had never occurred to Richard that our front door might be locked. Nor, obviously, to any of us. He had not bothered even to knock, or to call out to be let in.

We trusted our neighbors, and in all the years we lived together as a family on the mill hill, that never changed nor were there ever then any reasons to change. When change came abruptly, our father had not lived to see it, but Mother did. And when it happened, we marked the date in the calendars of our memory and we knew from that moment on, the doors on our street at Easley Mill would now be locked. Skeleton keys and the locks they matched would give way quickly to deadbolts and, in some cases, chain closures.

Thursday, December 23, 1999, had been a day so warm as to belie the fact that winter officially had begun. It was a shirtsleeve kind of a day under a bright sun, and family and friends soon were to begin arriving for all the Christmas festivities that always took place at Mother's house.

These Christmas gatherings had become a ritual for most of us, and a chance for us to revisit some of our warmest memories.

It was there, in the room that had been converted into a dining room, that my own childhood Christmas memories had been made, and they remain as cozy all these years later as the Warm Morning coal heater that once stood there on the hearth. It was in that room a long time ago, when I had been a believer in the magic of Santa, that I had heard while it was still dark on Christmas morning the restless whimpering coming from a box beneath the brightly decorated tree. The sounds told me that Santa had fulfilled my wish, a collie puppy whose name, Carlo, taken from my second grade reader, already had been chosen.

In the exciting anticipation of what the morrow would bring, Dad had told the three of us, when we were tucked in for the night, that we should sleep until it was daylight on Christmas morning. He knew, of course, that a full night's sleep was no option. Although it was still very dark when I first heard the sounds from the room beyond my door, I knew that sleep would come no more on this wonderful night. So I lay there, listening to that occasional whimper, and what seemed a scratching at a box, and watching my nearby window for the first signs of the glow of morning.

"That looks like daylight to me!" I shouted, not caring that the glow I saw at my window might be the product only of my imagination. I leaped from my bed and rushed to the nearby room.

All these years later, I still can remember the greeting from my new friend, and how surprisingly pleasant the breath of my puppy smelled as he lapped at my face for the first time. With white feet that seemed too large, he had that delightful awkwardness of a playful puppy. But he seemed all collie to me.

His nose already had much of the beautiful length of the breed and his coat perfectly matched the picture of the collie in the reading book. He was honey-colored with that soft collar of white across his shoulders and down his chest. A mere blaze of white between his beautiful eyes and onto his noble nose seemed to glow. The very tip of his tail was white and moved constantly.

Carlo was regal.

From the beginning, it was love such as I had never known before. But ours would be a bond quickly broken. Before Carlo could grow to adulthood, someone left fresh meat laced with poison for him to find, and I learned my first hard lesson about death. I also learned something about the ugly, sometimes dangerous side of life on the mill hill. I felt at the time, and still feel, that Carlo was something beautiful, and there lived among us on that mill hill a tortured soul determined to destroy such beauty. I never knew the name of the coward who did such a dastardly deed, though I had suspicions.

Mother discovered Carlo's still body in our front yard upon arriving home shortly after 11 p.m., after her eight hours of work on the second shift at the mill. And somehow she feared he had been poisoned. She hurried next door to awaken the Galloways.

Sleepily, Alvoid had answered the knocking at the door. "They've killed Wilton's dog," Mother said. "Better check to make sure your dog's all right."

Alvoid hurried to where his wonderful mixed-breed dog normally slept and found that he too had eaten the poison-laced meat and was in distress.

"Ina, bring the eggs!" Alvoid shouted to his wife. One by one, he hurriedly cracked perhaps a dozen eggs into a large pitcher and poured what he hoped would be an antidote down his dog's throat. Trembling from the desperation of trying to save his pet, Alvoid patted the dog lovingly on the head.

"If it wasn't too late, the eggs ought to do it," he said, more hopefully than instructive.

Alvoid had gotten to his dog in time. Within a day it was playful once again, none the worse for the ordeal. But our Carlo was gone.

The pain of that loss survives to this day.

Still, our Christmases were mostly happy times.

One of the happiest came just after the war had ended and the rationing of metal, rubber and some foodstuffs such as sugar no longer was in effect. I remember that I had kept my wish list simple. And I kept a secret; I no longer was sure that a fat man could make his way down our tiny chimney, but I knew it could be to my advantage to keep this doubt about whether Santa really existed from Mother and Dad. Not that they didn't know; it was just that if I had grown in such wisdom, there seemed no need to share the news in haste. The strategy paid off handsomely. Though mill wages were meager for Mother and Dad, there was under this cedar Christmas tree a shiny red and black J.C. Higgins bicycle with a tag bearing my name attached to the handlebar. The bicycle, surely the most expensive available in the Sears Roebuck catalog, was a thing of beauty. Twin headlights, real shock absorbers built into the front fork, a luggage rack, horn, mirrors left and right, mud flaps with reflectors, and raccoon tails streaming from each end of the handlebar. It was perfectly and fully equipped, which made it so heavy I would have to grow another two years before I had the strength to peddle it up even modest hills. But I loved that wonderful bicycle.

It didn't have a tail that wagged, and it didn't lick me in the face, but it also could not be killed the way my beloved Carlo had died.

And so, on what seemed a perfect day in December 1999, members of Mother's extended family soon were to gather to visit their own memories, almost all of them happy ones. Gathering at Mother's house had become a family tradition and extended to people who were not by blood or marriage listed on the family tree. By sundown on the eve of Christmas Eve, the house would be crowded. Since Dad had died all those years ago, no one went any more to search nearby farmland for the perfect cedar tree to stand in an honored place in the family home. I was grown before I discovered that not all Americans chose cedars as their Christmas trees, that spruces and some pines also serve the season well.

With Dad now gone, however, an artificial tree was carefully removed from storage and taken from its box instead early each December and placed in front of the large den window. It was a small tree which worked well; space was needed for stacks of gifts as members of the family and friends began arriving.

But in the early afternoon two days before Christmas, it was quiet at the end of Third Street save for the distant humming of a helicopter engine. The sound was so muted even it did not intrude, and no one was more than remotely aware that it even was there. Dee, one of Mother's granddaughters, had been the first to arrive bearing gifts, and the former school teacher sat slowly rocking in a chair in the distant corner of the den. Mother sat in her favorite recliner beside a table and lamp that separated her chair from one exactly like it in which Dad had been sitting that day, more than nine years earlier, reading his Bible.

Absently, Mother and Dee had watched the noon news on WYFF-TV and there had been a report of a double murder in the Georgetowne community near Easley.

"Where'd they say?" Mother, who had not been wearing her new hearing aid, asked Dee.

"In the Georgetowne community," Dee said, raising her voice to be clearly heard.

"That's not close to here," Mother said, seemingly relieved. "But ain't it awful, just two days before Christmas?"

Now the weather report was on the screen and they were calling for colder temperatures by Christmas Day. And everything seemed normal, a kind of quiet before the storm of loved ones arriving in the Christmas spirit. Mother pulled up her handmade comforter to provide additional warmth for her painfully arthritic shoulders, and settled in to await the arrival of the crowd.

She felt safe. Nice to be here, in this house, she thought. There had never been any reason to think any thoughts but wonderful ones on a day such as this. Except for the death of my beloved Carlo, the most serious challenge to the safety we felt in this place had come in my youth when we found a window screen torn and pushed aside. My savings, tucked away in a glass bank shaped like a pig and intended to buy a baseball glove I had seen at the Western Auto store in town, had been taken from its customary place on the nightstand beside my bed. Nothing else was missing, and we felt fortunate.

So on this spring-like day in the Christmas season of 1999, as was customary, no doors were locked. Mother and Dee sat there making small talk, wondering when Thomas, one of Mother's grandsons, might arrive on his long drive from the North Carolina Research Triangle. Or whether my sister Doris, Dee's mother, had been able to get away early from her work in Charlotte.

Peace and goodwill toward all men, however, was not being celebrated everywhere in our hometown. City and county police in the days to come would try to reconstruct the movements about town of a shadowy figure with blood on his hands. They came to believe that in the dark of the night before, a man drove his worn van past Glenwood Mill, along the street that parallels the railroad tracks, and then crossed the grade onto Easley's Main Street. He drove slowly along the deserted street and finally drew his vehicle into a parking space near Robinson's, a clothier that had been a long-time fixture in town, and within sight of Easley's new police station.

There, he must have stepped from the van and cautiously looked about. Much of Easley's business district already had moved east toward the U.S. 123 bypass that had been built years earlier. Still, the sidewalks would in a few hours be unusually busy with package-laden Christmas shoppers. For now, in the still of night, the streets were deserted. The man, a stranger in town, looked west along Main Street toward the Colony Theater, then east in the direction of the only major intersection in town, through which he had just driven. There the traffic light that managed the ebb and flow of vehicles on busy days now merely flashed a warning to proceed cautiously to anyone who might venture forth in the dark of night. Leaving his van behind, it is virtually certain that the stranger walked toward the intersection and the flashing traffic light. He moved along as best he could in the shadows cast by street lights and store illuminations.

There, where Williams' Grocery and Frierson's Drug Store once had done brisk business, the stranger turned right onto Pendleton Street. It was here that Saturday night dances were held in the 1950s, giving our preacher a chance to talk about "those dancing Methodists" in some of his Sunday sermons. The stranger's pace quickened and he looked about as if to see if anyone were following as he walked past the old bank, the place where the Winn-Dixie once stood, and past what had been Everett Bush's service station. He had left the downtown area behind and now approached Easley High School, then the band room that had opened when I had been a senior there, and past the football field.

There at the edge of the sleeping mill village, it is known that the stranger turned right onto Seventh Avenue. Houses built near Seventh Avenue lined the street on the left and the right and the stranger still walked cautiously. At the edge of the mill hill, he saw a house on the right that seemed abandoned. In the darkness, police believe, he climbed the steps to the front porch of the house where the Boggs family once had lived, looked cautiously into a window, and then tried the front door. It swung open and the stranger stepped inside. The place was empty.

He tried to move lightly across floors that creaked and found a place in a dark corner where he sat down, his back to the wall, facing the front door. He would remain here for a time, he apparently decided, and felt his trouser pockets to make sure a long-blade knife and a handgun still were quickly available if need be.

He must have tried to rest. It had been a long day and a long night for the stranger, and the thoughts surely swirled in his head. He perhaps tried to sleep, but it is doubtful that sleep would come. Still, he remained hidden away in an abandoned mill house. For the moment, at least, he must have felt safe. Chances are, he wondered if city and county police had yet spotted his van parked on Main Street, and whether anyone had seen him as he made his way through the night on foot.

Dawn came, and in the half light of the new day he could have seen, perhaps for the first time with certainty, the telltale traces of blood still on his hands. Slowly, so as not to draw attention from people living in nearby houses, he moved along the walls of the empty house toward a small room that seemed to be a bathroom. There, police would later learn, he twisted the faucet handle, hoping to wash some of the blood from his hands. No water came.

The stranger remained hidden away until the sun was high in a balmy Christmas season sky. By police reckoning, it now had been more than nine hours since he had abandoned his van on Main Street, plenty of time for law officers to have made the connection. The stranger decided that a fugitive on the move might be more difficult to track down, and in the full light of day he found the back door. What he could not have known is that police had been searching for him since long before dawn. At one time, the search was concentrated on the length of Pendleton Street from Main Street to WalMart just beyond U.S. 123, so that police on several occasions were within less than 100 feet of where he had found refuge in the empty house. But the search had proved fruitless, the expectation was that the man who had murdered the Otts had fled the area, and the manhunt had been called off in late morning.

Even the sound of helicopters buzzing about since first light came no more.

But the stranger knew only that he needed to remain as inconspicuous as possible and he considered his next move. The back of the house faced a now-empty parking lot for the high school and the football field just beyond. No one there to mark his movements.

Police had no difficulty putting together the rest of the stranger's journey once he descended the steps and made his way around the house on the side opposite that of the nearest neighbor. By now, traffic moved intermittently along Pendleton Street, but no one seemed to notice as the stranger once again stepped to Seventh Avenue and moved further into the mill hill, our mill hill.

There on his right was a home with, as usual, an open front door.

The stranger climbed the two steps to the porch and knocked on the door. Mrs. M.B. Merck, like Mother a widow living alone, searched the face of the stranger for some hint of recognition. None came.

"Sorry to bother you," the stranger offered, "but I wonder if you have some place I could wash my hands."

Mrs. Merck thought it a strange request, but she knew of no reason to deny the man so simple a plea. "Of course," she said, pushing open the thin screen door that separated the two people who had never before met. "Come on in." She pointed to the bathroom in the distance at the back of the house, an addition built many years earlier where the back porch once had been when indoor plumbing became available on the mill hill.

As the stranger entered the house, Mrs. Merck noticed a particular stain on his hands, and the thought of what the stain might be made her nervous. Instinctively, she knew she must not make the stranger aware of her suspicion.

In a few minutes, the stranger emerged from the bathroom and looked about quickly.

"Thank you very much," he said politely.

"You're certainly welcome," Mrs. Merck said, hoping, as she did, that the stranger would leave as quickly as he had come. The stranger stepped once again to the small front yard. She watched him go as he continued along Seventh Avenue.

Once the man was on his way, Mrs. Merck rushed to the telephone and dialed 911.

"This is 911. May I help you?" the voice on the other end of the line said.

"This is Mrs. M.B. Merck. I live on Seventh Avenue at Easley Mill," she reported. "A stranger just came to my door and asked if he could wash his hands. I'm not sure, but I think he had blood on his hands."

A few miles away, reserve Easley police officer Jack Brooks was completing his off-duty security shift at Conerstone Bank on the eastern edge of town.

Only one door away from the Merck home and across Seventh Avenue, the stranger could see the glow of a television set through the open door. He looked at his watch. Almost noon. He climbed the steps and knocked on the door. Edna Atkins, who was visiting with a neighbor, watched the man's arrival from where she sat in her living room. She rose to answer the knocking at the door.

"Hello," Ms. Atkins greeted the stranger. "You must be the grandson."

She knew that her next-door neighbor had been expecting the arrival of her grandson for a Christmas visit, and that she and her husband had just left to do some last-minute shopping. Now came a young man, a stranger, who surely must be the grandson, and certainly he could visit with her until the neighbors returned home.

"Won't you come in?" she said cheerily, pushing the screened door open. "They'll be home soon. This is one of my neighbors," she said in introduction to yet another mill hill resident who had stopped by for a visit.

The stranger entered and looked about. Ms. Atkins returned to her favorite chair, pointing to where the young man could sit while he waited. There on the coffee table before him was a copy of the December 22 *Greenville News*. The front page featured the apparent murder a day earlier of flower shop attendant Karen Hayden. Mrs. Hayden, 30 years old and the mother of two, had been found with her throat cut.

The stranger stared at the newspaper for a moment.

"Do you mind if I watch the noon news with you?" he finally asked Ms. Atkins.

"Certainly," she said, quickly switching the channel to WYFF-TV in Greenville. The news had just begun and the anchor newsman had opened with the report of a double murder in Easley. The stranger, seemingly entranced, watched.

"Authorities have identified the dead as Timothy and Sandra Ott, husband and wife, of the Georgetowne community near Easley," the announcer was saying in his business-as-usual detachment.

"They say what happened to the little boy yet?" the stranger asked.

"I haven't heard it," Ms. Atkins answered without an apparent second thought.

Now cameras zeroed in on the middle-class home where the shooting allegedly had taken place. "Authorities are looking for a white male in his late 20s. He was last seen driving a van with out-of-state license plates. He should be considered armed and very dangerous ..."

Soon, a picture of a weather map appeared on the television screen. "Turning colder by Christmas Day," a voice off-camera said. "Details after this."

"Thanks for letting me watch," the stranger said. To Ms. Atkins' surprise, the man she had assumed was her neighbor's grandson picked up the newspaper from the coffee table, tucked it under his arm and found his way to the door. Once again, he continued his walk along Seventh Avenue, moving deeper into the mill village. As he turned left onto Second Street, he could see, in the distance, a helicopter near the edge of the downtown area. It seemed gradually to be moving in his direction.

His pace grew even more rapid now as he passed the house where Paul Waldrop, once a uniformed police officer, had lived. He continued past the vacant lot where the Waters home had stood until it burned to the ground one cold winter night, past where the Coxes had lived. They once had owned a wonderful dog, mostly collie, which would meet me at 4 o'clock each morning and walk with me around my paper route, occasionally placing himself between me and other strange and perhaps threatening dogs. He continued past what had been the home of Bess White and, across the street, the house in which the Tinsleys, including sons Neal and Ballard, had lived. In the 1940s, the Tinsleys were known as the best builders of iron-wheeled wagons on the mill hill. Theirs stood out and featured steering wheels that actually worked. "It's all in the way the leather straps are wrapped around the broomstick we use for the steering column," Neal once told me as though he were revealing a family secret.

Finally, the stranger had come to the end of Second Street and the sound of a helicopter engine seemed to grow louder. He climbed the steps to the front porch of the last house on the right, where Aunt Nan Ledford used to live. She wasn't our aunt, but she was someone's aunt, and for as long as she and her husband, who bore the emotional scars of having fought in World War I, had lived there, she was Aunt Nan to us.

The stranger knocked on the door. There was no response. He tried again and listened closely now for any indication of movement inside the house. Still, it was quiet.
Now he tried the door. It was unlocked. He looked cautiously about and stepped inside.

He sat down at the kitchen table and for perhaps 15 minutes he remained there, waiting, listening. The sound of the helicopter had faded away. He looked about the kitchen. Christmas cards someone had been addressing, despite the late pre-holiday date, still sat neatly stacked beside the box in which they had been kept. An ink pen lay beside the cards.

The stranger wondered who these people were who lived here. Were they young and strong? Probably not, he decided. Everything and everyone in this community seemed to be older. Still, he decided not to wait despite the fact that for the moment he felt safe.

He drew from the stack on the table a Christmas card that had neither been signed nor addressed. Picking up the pen, he began writing:

"My mind is a whirling mess of emotion and sadness," Dallen Bounds scribbled. "I was a mad man. God forgive me. I never hurt anyone or any thing unless in protection. I don't know what happened last night. I really don't. I'm so alone. Forgive me, Sandi. I love you. What were we doing? Why did I do this? I'm sorry."

# Come Quittin' Time

Leaving the card on which he had written behind, he departed the way he had come and faintly in the distance he could hear once again the distinctive sound of a helicopter engine. The very presence of the helicopter flying in low circles in the distance told the stranger that his van had been discovered parked along Main Street. He knew nothing of Mrs. Merck's call to the police. The police had theorized that if the killer they sought had reached U.S. 123, he could have perhaps quickly escaped. From there, Greenville was but 20 minutes away and, going west could eventually take him to Atlanta where becoming lost in a crowd would be an easy task.

In a rush now, the stranger turned right within sight of U.S. 123, no more than 300 yards away, and hurried up the small hill toward the end of Third Street.

# Chapter Nine

## *Dark Christmas*

The stranger knew none of the history of this place or about the lives of the people who had made up this community when the mill in the distance hummed through most of a century. Nor did he care. He had no idea that this always had been a place of peace and safety, of neighbors caring for neighbors. Or that the people who lived on the mill hill when he arrived in the closing days of the 20th century were old weavers and spinners and such. They were good people living out their days on Social Security and, for some, the meager monthly checks of cotton mill pensions.

The place had changed, the changes coming so gradually that almost no one noticed. There where the Smiths once lived, for example, were the Burketts, grown brother and sister, and their parents. Mother had never even spoken with Karl Burkett, the son and brother, in all the time they had been her neighbors. Karl Burkett seemed a solitary sort of man. There were days he would go to the mailbox without once acknowledging the presence of neighbors in their yards. No greetings. No talk of the weather. No asking about grandchildren.

None of that mattered to the stranger, or that he himself was an intruder, as he hurried along. What he saw there on the right was a different looking mill house, one with a brick wing that obviously had been added to a small dwelling. Even from a distance, the stranger could see that only the storm door at the back of the wing was closed. The lights of a Christmas tree glistened in the window. He looked about. He saw no one who could mark his coming or, perhaps, his going.

He walked even more briskly now. He opened the gate in the chain link fence and hurried across a small patio that served as a porch. He quickly opened the storm door, stepped inside, and took a seat in the chair that had been that of my father, the place he sat reading his Bible on the day he died.

Mother smiled at the man and once more turned her attention to the television where a Christmas special now was being shown. Dee merely continued to gently rock. Indeed, it was not unusual for new friends of various family members to find their ways to Mother's house at Christmastime. On what had been a perfect day, mother assumed that this young man, who seemed to be no older than Dee, was one of her granddaughter's friends. At the same time, Dee decided silently that the man sitting across the way was a member of Mother's church who had been invited to enjoy the holiday season in this house. Neither scenario would have been unusual and there was no obvious reason to think otherwise.

So, for a time the three people sat there saying nothing until Mother finally spoke.

"Dee, aren't you going to introduce me to your friend?" she said.

"Ma-mar," said Dee, using the pet name by which she and her sister, Sherri, knew mother, "I thought he was somebody from your church."

Mother turned and looked closely at the stranger in Dad's chair.

"Who are you?" she asked.

The stranger did not immediately answer. "Is anybody else here?" he finally asked.

"No, just us," Mother answered, not yet alarmed.

The stranger arose, looked nervously about, and closed and locked the solid wood door to the patio he had just crossed as he had arrived. He returned to the recliner. Dee felt her heart racing at the strange behavior. She and Mother were about to learn that there indeed was danger about.

"They're coming for me," he said in a matter-of-fact tone. "I've been in prison and I'll never go back there. I'll kill myself before I'll go back to prison. They've been looking for me for a while because of what happened this morning. I've killed two people. And I've got a couple of other warrants out for me in other states, too."

"We've got a garage out back," Mother responded. "You could hide in there." The garage had been built across town at Glenwood Mill in the late 1940s to protect my Uncle J.C.'s new Pontiac which we all had gone to see when he bought it. By the early 1950s, J.C. no longer needed the garage, so it was moved intact on a flatbed truck to our yard, and there it stood, mostly empty now except for a scattering of garden tools my father had used.

"It'd be a good place to hide," Mother said as she tried to come up with a way to get this man once again out of her house.

"No!" the stranger cut her off sharply.

For a time, no one spoke. Mother and Dee were shocked at what they had been told. Were they in the company of a serial killer?

"Have you been watching the news?" he asked, breaking the heavy silence. Now Mother remembered the noon news report of the double murder near Easley. The names of the dead had not been familiar to her, but now a chill such as she had never known gripped her body.

"I meant to kill him," the stranger said coldly, "but I didn't mean to kill her." Now tears welled in his tired-looking eyes. "I wonder what'll happen to the little boy." A five-year-old named Grant had been left an orphan as he slept through the violence of the night.

The stranger was silent for a time once again, and then turned to where Mother sat in her favorite recliner. "What's that for?" he demanded, pointing to a First Alert medallion Mother had worn about her neck for most of 10 years.

"That's her Lifeline," Dee answered quickly, before Mother had a chance to speak.

"What's it do?" he pressed.

"If she has a medical emergency or if she falls, she can press the button and get help," Dee answered truthfully.

Now the stranger stood up yet again, drew a long-blade knife from his pocket and reached toward Mother. The light from the picture window beyond the shining Christmas tree shimmered on the cold polished steel blade and she turned away, tightly closing her eyes, fearing an assault. "Will this be the moment I die?" she thought to herself.

But he reached the blade of the knife toward the lanyard that held Mother's Lifeline in place about her neck, and as he did, Dee could see the grip of a handgun in his pocket. Suddenly, she could feel her own fear growing to almost an uncontrollable level. With a quick flick of the razor-like blade, he cut the lanyard holding the Lifeline in place, and put Mother's link to the medical world in his pocket.

Frightened, but not yet fully aware of the mortal danger she could yet face, Mother pushed her comforter aside and rose from her recliner. Always a fighter, Mother seemed suddenly defiant. Dee, already emotionally dealing with the seriousness of the moment, mustered the courage she did not feel, and spoke to her grandmother in a pointed, challenging manner unlike any exchange the two women had ever had.

"Sit down, Ma-mar!" she sternly ordered her beloved grandmother. Surprisingly, Mother obediently settled once again into her recliner.

And now there was silence once more between the stranger and the two women. The minutes seemed to drag. The distinctive sounds of a helicopter grew alternately louder and then faded to nothingness, and each time it came it seemed to underscore yet again the magnitude of the danger the two women faced. Dee was the first to speak.

"We're expecting some of our relatives at any time," Dee announced. "What happens when they get here?"

"They'll just have to join us," he said menacingly.

Now Dee's mind was racing. She alone knew without question that the stranger had come armed with more than a single knife, though Mother by now feared that the blade before which she had cringed perhaps was not his only weapon. Dee tried to remember everything she had ever read, every piece of advice she had ever heard for surviving nightmares such as this, and she remembered someone - she couldn't remember who - talking about the importance of trying to bond with an intruder. Dee rationalized that perhaps she and her beloved grandmother had nothing to lose.

"What's your name?" Dee asked. She was surprised how calm her own voice had seemed as the words came out. So calm, in fact, that even the stranger seemed to relax.

"Dallen Bounds," he answered in an equally surprisingly even, conversational tone of voice. "I use several names, but Dallen Bounds is my real name. I've been driving a van that's registered in another name. When I was in Arizona, I heard about an eight-year-old boy who had died, and I just took his name. That's the name that's on the van. I use other names, too."

Earlier, when it was still dark, police had found the van registered to Terry Joe Darnell, but did not yet know that the name was the same as that of a dead eight-year-old boy engraved on an Arizona tombstone.

Without her hearing aid, Mother could understand only parts of the conversation between Dee and the stranger. But she understood the intentions of her granddaughter whom she knew so well. She knew that Dee was trying to calm a potentially deadly situation. Mother decided to join in the attempt.

"Would you like for me to pray for you?" she asked the stranger. "You know, God will forgive you if you truly repent, even if you have murdered, and I'll be happy to pray for you if you like."

Mother's voice, like Dee's, was so calm that the calmness soothed even her.

"I've been praying all morning," he answered, his eyes once again welling.

"God loves you. If you ask him to, and you are truly sorry for your sins, He will forgive you and no matter what has happened, or will happen, you will have that forgiveness," Mother said, then fell silent once again. She relaxed in the calmness she felt though she understood the danger. She too wanted to keep the dangerous stranger talking.

"What time did those people die?" she asked, taking a chance, choosing a subject the stranger perhaps had no intention of discussing.

"I guess it was 1:30, maybe 2 o'clock in the morning," he answered in a matter-of-fact manner, his voice still surprisingly even.

"And you've been on the run ever since?" Mother asked.

"Yes, m'am," he said.

"You must be very hungry."

"Pretty hungry," he confirmed.

"We had some cubed steak and onion gravy for lunch and there's still a lot left," Mother said. "I'd be happy to fix some and cook some biscuits for you if you'd like."

"Yes, m'am," he said again. "I'd like that."

"The trouble is, I'll have to go into the kitchen to fix the biscuits. Is that all right?"

The stranger nodded his approval and mother once again pushed away the comforter that had kept her arthritic shoulders warm and started to the kitchen nearby. As she passed the stranger, his words seemed no longer as calm and as even as they had.

"Remember," he said, biting his words and clutching her arm roughly, demanding her attention. "I'll be watching you."

Mother felt an involuntary shiver at the back of her neck, but said nothing more as she continued to the kitchen.

More noisily than she could ever remember, Mother removed the old, worn wooden dough bowl from the place where she had kept it since my Father added a two-room wing to our four-room mill house years earlier. She clanged dishes, hoping that somehow someone would hear the commotion, know that so much clatter was not like Mother, and would come to inquire.

No one came.

Praying was not an activity to which Mother was ever a stranger. She once prayed over every seed she planted in a garden. The result was such a bountiful harvest that Mother and Dad were very weary of collecting vegetables and filling the freezers of all their relatives and many of their neighbors by the time the last okra pod was plucked from its stalk.

"Be careful what you pray for," she said, using the garden experience as a cautionary example of the power of prayer. "You might get it."

Now, Mother knew what she would be praying for.

"Lord, help us," she prayed out loud, though softly. "Send somebody to help us, dear Lord."

"What's she saying?!" asked the suddenly alarmed stranger sitting in the room with Dee only less than a dozen feet from where Mother was busy with a meal preparation. "Who's she talking to?"

"She's praying," Dee responded in a scolding tone of voice. That Mother would pray came as no surprise to Dee who also had offered her own prayers silently since the stranger arrived. "You're scaring her to death and she's praying. She's afraid of you."

Praying as she went, Mother hurried about the kitchen preparing fresh dough, turning the oven on and adjusting baking temperatures, checking on the cubed steak she had offered making sure it still was warm and that there was enough gravy.

Now she was pouring just the right amount of flour into the mixing bowl, though she never measured to be precise.

"Lord, send someone to help us," she implored yet again. "Send Thomas." Thomas was expected to be among the first arrivals at the end of a long drive from Durham, North Carolina, where he was a computer specialist. Thomas would know what to do, whom to call, how to handle this situation, she thought.

Then another thought came, and her fright grew to almost uncontrollable levels: It was likely that the first male to arrive would die, she reasoned.

"Oh, Lord, don't send Thomas," she pleaded even more earnestly now. "If you send Thomas, he might get killed. But, please, Lord, send somebody!"

By now, the stranger no longer was alarmed by the prayerful voice in the nearby kitchen. His attention had been diverted to the television where a Christmas show still was being shown. His gaze was riveted on the cheerful holiday scenes depicted in the television special. He seemed transfixed. Dee

117

wondered how long it had been since this man had felt the true spirit of the season.

Again and again, Mother squeezed the soft dough from her hands and formed perfect biscuits and patted them gently onto the baking sheet leaving the indentations of the knuckles on her right hand as she always had. When Dad was alive, Mother had always made her biscuits on the thin side because that's the way Dad liked them best, and she still made them that way though he had been gone for nine years.

Checking to make sure the oven was fully heated, Mother opened the door and slid the sheet of biscuits onto the rack. She hurried to the kitchen sink to wash the flour and fresh dough from her hands, just as she had done thousands of times, but never in moments as stressful as this. As she did, she looked out the kitchen window yet again. Still, no help in sight. She renewed her prayers.

The Christmas show that had so captured the attention of the stranger was still casting its spell. But Mother could be heard placing a dish and silverware there at the end of the kitchen table.

The stranger pulled himself away from the TV, stood and walked toward the fireplace and studied the faces in family photos displayed in an array of frames on the mantle.

"Who are all these people?" he asked Dee.

Dee arose from her chair and joined the stranger before the fireplace. One by one, she identified the faces in the pictures, occasionally offering interesting asides about some of her relatives, as though she were talking to a specially invited guest who had a genuine interest in the Browning family.

Then Dee came to the last picture of my Father ever taken. It had been an oppressively hot summer day and the hint of perspiration from work in his garden which he had just finished still could be seen on his face. The bottom two buttons on his knit shirt were fastened, but the neck was pushed open on the sticky, hot day. He had smiled broadly when Tammy, his granddaughter who had snapped the picture, had called his attention to the camera.

"That's Granddad," Dee said softly, not hiding her love for her grandfather. "He sat in that chair where you've been sitting reading his Bible on the day he died, just like he did every day. He got up and told Ma-mar he'd see her later, drove himself to the hospital and died."

"When did that happen?" the stranger asked.

"August 1990."

"Were they married for a long time?"

"Fifty-five, 56 years," Dee said, trying to make quick calculations in her memory.

"Think of that," the stranger said. "That's a long time to be married to one person. Do you think they were happy?"

"I *know* they were happy," Dee said without qualification and without hesitation. For the first time since the frightening ordeal had begun, Dee allowed a soft smile to play across her lips.

The stranger now removed Mother's Lifeline once again from his pocket and he tried to tie a tiny knot in the lanyard, seeking to make it whole again where he had cut it from her neck. "Your grandmother's a very nice lady," he said as he pulled strength into the small knot he finally had made. "I shouldn't have cut this from her neck."

Now his mood suddenly changed yet again. Tears came to his eyes and he did not bother to brush them away.

"I didn't mean to kill her," he said, now giving voice to his own torment and the double murder from which he had been fleeing for most of a dozen hours. The female victim had been his girlfriend, he said, and the two of them had planned the murder of her husband. "She just got in the way," he sobbed.

"I'm sorry," said Dee softly, expressing an emotion she wasn't sure she felt nor that she should be feeling under the circumstances.

"We were going to get married," he said, looking once again at the pictures of Mother and Dad on the mantle. "We wanted to be together. She had a five-year-old son. What do you suppose is going to happen to him now?"

"The little boy will be taken care of," Dee assured the stranger. The sobs shook his shoulders. He wept quietly for what seemed a long time. And finally the tears stopped coming.

"I don't want to die here," he said, his voice now breaking with emotion. "This is such a nice house, you're such nice people and you've got such nice neighbors. I know. I stopped at three houses on the way here and two of them let me right in. Nice people. The other people weren't home."

Mother had remained in the kitchen, busying herself with preparations for a meal for the stranger. But Dee understood that her grandmother was contemplating an escape. On two occasions, Mother had appeared in a corner of the kitchen visible only to Dee and had nodded indicating that she was considering making a run hopefully to the safety of some neighboring house. Twice, with unspoken words, with only a look, Dee had sternly declined. Dee knew she still was aware of something Mother did not know with certainty, that the stranger not only carried a very sharp knife, he also had a handgun in his pocket.

She knew it was not likely that either could escape if a run to safety were attempted. And Dee knew beyond question now that this man had killed at least two people and had nothing more to lose in adding two innocent women to the count.

What Dee could not have known was that Timothy Ott also had decided to attempt to flee in the dark of night to the hopeful safety of a neighbor's home as the menacing stranger hunted him down. But Ott had been gunned down in the foyer of a neighbor's house while the home owner, home alone with her husband out of town, cowered traumatized in a closet and out of sight.

Dee was not certain that she could, with looks alone, restrain Mother's attempt at flight for much longer. She searched her mind for a way out.

"The trailer!" she thought. Years earlier, Mother and Dad had shared the purchase of 10 acres of land a few miles away in the country with my sister, Marlene. There, Mother and Dad had set up a small mobile home and had cleared close to a half acre for a garden.

"Maybe I can get him out of the house and to the trailer, then Ma-mar would be safe," Dee reasoned. Dee knew that she might not survive such a plan, but it was a chance she was willing to take. Boldly, she offered the plan to the stranger.

"You know, Ma-mar has a trailer up in the country toward Table Rock and that'd be a good place for you to hide out," she said.

"You think I'd be all right there?" he asked.

"I think so."

Praying as she moved about, Mother had retreated out of sight once again and now leaned against the kitchen sink and tried to come up with a viable escape plan. Once again she looked about the neighborhood from the kitchen window. Karl Burkett, the not-so-friendly man who now lived in the house where the Smiths had been for so many years, was walking down his steps and going to the mailbox at the street.

Perhaps this was her chance, Mother thought, and began frantically, though silently, waving, trying to get her neighbor's attention. His sister, Mary, whom Mother had gotten to know, and their father also had stepped from the house and waited while Karl reached into the mailbox. For some reason, he then turned and for the first time Mother had ever known him to, looked toward her kitchen window. He stopped in his tracks when he saw Mother's frantic waving, then began to cross the street toward the short walkway leading to Mother's screened front porch.

By now, the stranger had settled once again into Dad's recliner and had become engrossed anew in the Christmas show on television. He did not notice when Mother hurried from the kitchen, through the corner of the living room and onto the front porch to meet Karl Burkett. Dee knew something was happening, though she did not yet know exactly what was taking place. She carefully watched Dallen Bounds for fear that he too would hear the commotion and perhaps react violently.

"Go call 911," Mother said desperately, but still trying not to speak too loudly, as Burkett came closer.

Across the street, Mary Burkett and her father, both of whom knew of Mother's ailments and that she had undergone open heart surgery, heard Mother's plea to call 911. The elder Mr. Burkett quickly rushed back into his house and dialed the number. He wondered how ill Mother had become.

"My name's Burkett and I live at the end of Third Street at Easley Mill," he told the 911 operator. "Mrs. Browning, my neighbor across the street, needs an ambulance. Please hurry."

"They're on their way," the operator reported.

The call also had further alerted the police who were searching for Bounds and who were monitoring all 911 calls as part of that effort. They had already determined that any call for an ambulance or any other form of medical assistance south of Main Street would call for a police response as well.

By now, Dee had heard enough of what was going on outside to become alarmed. But the stranger still was transfixed by the Christmas show on television and now a familiar holiday song, a part of the show, was coming from the television.

"Oh, Dallen," Dee called out, speaking more loudly than usual, "that's my all-time favorite Christmas song. Do you mind if I turn up the volume a little so I can hear it better?"

"Not at all," Bounds said agreeably.

Dee pushed the volume button on the remote control and the sound began to build until it was unusually loud, just loud enough to drown out the voices from the front of the house where Karl Burkett was trying to determine if a true emergency existed.

"What did you say?" he asked as he drew close to the house.

"I need you to call 911," pleaded Mother who did not know that a call already had been made. "There's a murderer in my house and my granddaughter and I might get killed."

Burkett, who had never spoken with Mother until this moment, considered the possibility that all of this was merely the ravings of an elderly woman suffering from dementia. But he could not be certain.

"You say there's a killer in the house?" Burkett pressed.

"He's already murdered two people and he might kill us. Please hurry and call 911," Mother begged. Fearing that the stranger might become violent if he realized she was no longer in the kitchen, Mother turned and rushed back into the house.

But instead of retreating and hurrying to a phone, Karl Burkett was on her heels and together the two hurried into the kitchen where loud Christmas music from the nearby den was filling the rooms now.

Burkett went to the edge of the kitchen and looked into the den where the stranger sat, his back to Burkett, still engrossed in the Christmas show. Dee, still in her chair in the corner of the den, now turned to look at the neighbor from across the street, a look of terrifying fear on her face.

He understood without question.

As rapidly as he had come, Burkett retraced his steps and hurried from the house without Bounds having ever known of his presence. Burkett rushed across the street and into his own living room.

"Call 911 for Mrs. Browning," he ordered his sister.

"Dad's already called 'em," she announced. "The ambulance is on the way."

"She doesn't need an ambulance. Call them back and tell them she needs the police. There's a murderer in her house."

Quickly, Mary redialed the three-digit emergency number.

"We called a minute ago to get an ambulance to Mrs. Browning's," she explained. "She doesn't need the ambulance. She needs the police. There's a killer in her house."

The police dispatcher suddenly had uncharacteristic difficulty in finding an available patrol. But reserve police officer Jack Brooks had just arrived at police headquarters, barely a block from where Bounds in the dark of night had parked his van. He was asked to respond to the 911 call at the end of Third Street.

Brooks hurried to his squad car at about the same time Easley policeman Brad Stansell picked up the request for a response to the mill hill. He also wheeled his squad car around and headed for Third Street.

# Chapter Ten

*No Place to Run*

Alone once again in the kitchen now, Mother knew she could only wait. "Dear Lord, we are in your hands. Please help us. Make the police hurry," she prayed once again. She stirred heat once more into the cubed steak still warming slowly on the stove and reached into the oven and brought out a sheet of golden brown biscuits. The smell of the freshly baked bread wafted through the house.

"You hungry?" Mother called out in all the cheerfulness she could muster.

The stranger pulled himself away from the show on television. "Yes, m'am," he answered, his own response sounding more cheerful than he felt.

"It'll be on the table in just a minute," Mother said.

Dee thought how much the exchange sounded little different from any Mother might have with any of her children, or any of her visitors.

Now, the sound of a helicopter engine came again, and this time the sound meant something. God, Mother said to herself, was answering her prayer.

"OK, here's your lunch," she reported.

A glass of iced tea awaited the stranger and the biscuits were sending curls of steam into the air as he sat down in the very chair that once had been our father's at the end of the table. He reached into his pocket, and the two women held their breath. He drew out the Lifeline he had cut earlier from Mother's neck. Holding it as though it were a hostess gift, he handed it once again to Mother.

"I'm sorry I took this from you," he apologized.

Speechless now, Mother held the pendant that had long been her emergency lifeline cupped in both hands.

Dee knew it still was important that she keep the stranger's attention. Joining him in the kitchen, she now once again mentioned the mobile home in the country that Dad had loved so much.

"It's about five miles out in the country. It's a mobile home surrounded by trees. You'd be safe there."

Clearly, the stranger was interested. He listened.

"If you would like, I'll drive you up there after you eat. But you'd have to let Ma-mar go," she said. "It would be a good place for you to hide out."

"I'll think about it," he said.

Mother placed the steaming hot biscuits before him and placed the perfectly cooked cubed steak smothered in onion gravy on his plate.

"Looks good," he approved. But something had gotten his attention and he looked startled. He too had for the first time in some time heard the sound of an approaching helicopter.

Once again, Dee felt a sickening chill creep back into her senses. Her intuition told her that this crisis was near an end, and that it could end tragically for her grandmother as well.

"The trailer," she said to the stranger, urgency in her voice as the sound of the helicopter grew louder. "I'll drive you up there right now if you'll let Ma-mar go."

He quickly nodded agreement.

Mother turned and beyond the kitchen window she could see two police cars arriving. Both moved silently and without lights flashing and sirens blaring. As she watched, trying not to alarm the dangerous stranger, Mother saw more police cars approaching in the distance. One policeman ran past the kitchen window, but Bounds was facing the wrong way to have seen. Suddenly uniformed officers and plainclothes policemen were swarming, taking positions so that the house obviously was surrounded. There would be no further escape now for the stranger. It was too late for a trip to the mobile home in the countryside that Dee had offered. Dee moved quickly, returning to the den. Newly arriving officers quietly warned curious neighbors, including the Burketts, to safety and out of sight.

"We had three choices," Brooks said years later. "Brad and I could have split up and covered the house front and back. But that would probably mean that both women would die.

"We could wait, and maybe have the same result. Or, the two of us could go right away."

The two policemen arrived quietly at the same decision, and now officer Brooks, who had been off duty, was suddenly aware that he had arrived at this potentially volatile scene without the security of his bulletproof vest. Stansell wore his.

Through the den window, Stansell could see Dee clearly separated from where the stranger sat at the kitchen table. Brooks saw Mother at the same instant that she saw him. She realized the ordeal was about to reach its conclusion, and she hurried quickly from the kitchen toward the living room. "All we needed to decide then was which of us would go high (standing), and which would go low (kneeling)," Brooks said. Even that decision was made quickly with no words being spoken. "If we had gone rushing in and he had that girl (Dee) as a shield, she probably would have died, and so would we," Brooks said.

A backup force was rapidly assembling. But Brooks and Stansell knew that this would be resolved only by two uniformed officers, the two of them. Saying nothing, even to each other, officers Brooks and Stansell acted quickly. Suddenly, there were heavy footsteps on the front porch. Mother heard the steps and moved even more rapidly now, hurrying on toward the distant bedroom. She had briefly encountered officers Brooks, with Stansell close behind, and pointed silently toward the kitchen as she went, seeking refuge as far removed as she could get. On her way, she passed yet another police officer who had entered by an unlocked back door.

She wanted to stop and hug him, but realized that now was not the time for rejoicing.

Bounds was now trapped.

He had just picked up his fork to begin his meal, and had looked up and into the face of officer Stansell standing near the end of the table with Brooks, ironically the son of Nettie Brooks, one of Mother's closest friends, kneeling to Stansell's right. Both had handguns trained on Bounds. There was no escaping.

"What the....!" Bounds exclaimed and in a flash had drawn the handgun Dee had spotted early on from his pocket and placed it to his temple.

"No! Don't!" Brooks shouted, as he heard a telltale click of the handgun. Brooks' shout was drowned out by the report and the recoil of the deadly weapon that Bounds had placed to his right temple.

Both officers had been prepared to fire if the muzzle of Bounds' handgun had started to point forward; instead, with his head slightly bowed, he had placed it to his own head.

Dee stood traumatized at the grizzly scene. Mother had heard the sound of the one shot and since she had never been certain that the stranger had come armed with a gun assumed, in error, that sound had come from the firearm of one of the policemen.

She trembled, and her hands were shaking as she put them to her face. "Oh, Lord, why'd they have to shoot that man?" she prayed.

The prayerful question had barely been spoken when Dee screamed from the den, "Oh, Ma-mar, he killed himself!"

Dee then reached for the telephone that was in its place on the lamp table between the two recliners in the den.

"Put the phone down!" a newly arrived police officer ordered. "Don't touch anything."

"You don't understand," Dee responded. "I *must* call my grandmother's daughter. She needs to be here with her mother right now." Ignoring the order, Dee dialed the number.

Marlene was sitting at her kitchen table visiting with her son, Thomas, who had just arrived from North Carolina. She reached for the ringing phone.

"Hello," she said.

"Marlene, a man just killed himself in Ma-mar's house."

Marlene thought Dee was telling a joke, as was typical with her, and she waited for the punch line for only a moment. "Dee," she scolded her niece. "That's not funny."

"Aunt Marlene," Dee said, her voice now trembling with emotion. "This is not a joke. A murderer came in here and held us hostage for a while, and when the police got here, he killed himself."

Suddenly, Marlene viewed it as no joke.

"I'll be right there," Marlene responded. She and Thomas sped the two miles from her house to the mill village. There she hurried from Thomas' car to her Mother's house, but was stopped by a police officer before she could enter.

"You can't go in there," he said.

"I *have* to go in there. My mother's in there and she needs me," Marlene argued.

"Who are you?" inquired the officer, speaking softly now.

"I'm Marlene Burke, her older daughter."

"Your mother's across the street. I'll have a lady officer go over there with you."

The two women hurried up the steps and into the Burkett home where detectives were questioning the two badly shaken women. Greg Smith, Dee's close friend who had arrived for the Christmas gathering at Mother's house only minutes after the shot rang out, also was directed to the neighbor's house. He held Dee's hand and sought to comfort her, and already he realized how close he perhaps had come to being involved in the violent final scene in Mother's kitchen. Marlene hurried to Mother and placed her hand on Mother's shoulder to comfort her. Marlene could feel the trembling to Mother's core.

"Excuse me just a minute," Marlene said as she interrupted the detective in his questioning. "Mother, everything's OK now. You're safe and I need you to take a big breath and relax as much as you can."

Mother breathed deeply and exhaled. Marlene could feel the trembling subside, though only slightly.

"Again, Mother," she said softly, reassuringly. Again, Mother breathed deeply and exhaled, and the trembling began to lose its grip.

Nearby, the questioning of Dee had taken an unexpected turn.

"What did you say his name was?" the detective asked.

"Bounds," she answered. "Dallen Bounds."

"And how long have you known Dallen Bounds?"

"I never saw the man until today," Dee, somewhat taken aback, answered sharply.

Within minutes, the detective would return yet again to inquire if there had been an ongoing relationship between Dee and Bounds. This time, Dee had no opportunity to answer.

"Detective," Marlene said pointedly. "I can tell you that there's no way Dee would have known this man until today. He came into my Mother's house and could have killed the two of them and they're just lucky to be alive. That's all there was to it."

Now came the lonesome, sad wail of the ambulance's siren as it roared down Third Street and disappeared on its run to the hospital with the apparent remains of Dallen Bounds.

For Mother, there was one more horror to endure.

"I'm tired," Mother announced. "I'm going to go home and rest."

"I'm sorry, Mrs. Browning, but you can't go home," the detective said as gently as he could.

"What do you mean I can't go home? It's my house. It's has been my home for almost 60 years. And I can't go to my own house?"

"No, m'am," the officer said firmly, sympathy in his voice. "We cannot allow you inside now because your home has become a crime scene."

"How long will I have to stay away?" asked Mother, on the verge of tears because the place she wanted most to be was in her own home, in what until this day had always been her own sanctuary.

"It will be several hours," he said softly. "We will see that you are comfortable."

It would be most of seven hours before Mother would be permitted back into her home.

With a murderer no longer in the house and the crime scene investigation in full swing, newsmen were on the scene,

131

taking pictures and shooting film of the wonderful home at the end of Third Street where, until this day, no one ever had come truly as a stranger.

"We are confident that this was the man responsible for the murders early this morning in the Georgetowne community," a police sergeant was telling the gathered writers and broadcasters.

"No," he said, answering another question. "He was the only suspect. We are confident that the murders have been solved."

"What is the man's condition?" one of the reporters asked.

"Not good," the sergeant answered. "We're not sure he's going to make it."

Dallen Bounds, a stranger, was pronounced dead at Palmetto Baptist Medical Center on the north side of Easley.

Police officer Brooks, who had had Dallen Bounds in his own gun sights, assisted with the investigation, then found a phone himself. He placed a call to his mother, Nettie.

"Just wanted to tell you to be sure to watch the 6 o'clock news," he told his mother on the phone. "Your buddy, Martha Browning, has gone through an ordeal today and it'll be all over the news."

His mother had wanted to know how her friend was doing under the trying circumstances. "She's great," he reported in the phone conversation. "She was just as calm as she could be. In fact, she was asking me questions, like what was my name. When I told her my name was Brooks, she asked if I knew you.

"I told her, 'She's my mother,' and she told me you were one of her best friends. So, she's doing fine. It's amazing how calm Mrs. Browning is."

Brooks and Stansell returned to police headquarters where they filed their own incident reports.

"The chaplain is here if you need to go talk to him," the Police Chief William D. Traber told Brooks when he presented his report.

"I don't need to see the chaplain," Brooks responded.

"Do you need anything?" Traber asked.

"A cook," he smiled. "I'm hungry."

Brooks dined on a meal of hamburger with French fries and ketchup.

"If the man had been somebody else, I might have felt differently," said Brooks, a fulltime special education teacher in the Pickens County public school system. "But we knew he already had killed two people and it turned out to be more than that. When he killed himself, it didn't bother me.

"There were a number of ways this could have ended up, most of them very tragic. The way it ended was the best of all possibilities. God certainly must have had a hand in that."

In the days ahead, Bounds also would be considered the likely suspect in the deaths in Greenville of two sales people in separate incidents, one in June 2002 in which 26-year-old salesman Jonathan Lara was found dead in a RadioShack store, and the other the flower shop murder a day before he arrived at Mother's house. At the RadioShack scene, there had been marked similarities to the later flower shop killing. Lara had been found lying in the floor, still tied to the chair in which he had died, his throat slashed by a very sharp knife. Forensic analysis would link the knife with which Bounds cut the lanyard from Mother's neck with the murder at the RadioShack six months earlier. Bounds would become a "person of interest" in more than one unsolved murder in the western United States.

There had been so many similarities in the RadioShack and the flower shop murders that Greenville police worried that they were looking for a serial killer.

In the coming days, police would discover that Bounds had left behind a long list of criminal activities and had warrants for his arrest pending in Arizona, and that he had arrived in South Carolina in December 1997.

In ten years, he had worked at nine different jobs and had served several short prison sentences for burglary, domestic violence, interference with judicial procedures and driving while impaired. He had worked as a landscaper, a customer service representative, a store clerk, a heating technician, a seafood distributor, a janitor, a beer distributor and had laid cable and stocked shelves. He also had been a meat cutter.

Bounds graduated without distinction from Timberline High School near Olympia, Washington and, in the years since, had briefly studied at a seminary and at a beauty school.

During the Thanksgiving holiday in 1999, he had delivered hot meals to shut-in senior citizens in Greenville.

When police inspected the apartment Bounds shared with Casandra Cae Laster, who was charged as an accessory after the fact of murder in the RadioShack killing, they found various witchcraft and white supremacist literature. A framed and matted picture of a lynching hung prominently on his bedroom wall. Among his reading material was a Ku Klux Klan bible.

In 1997, Bounds had driven across country apparently with no particular destination in mind though he would wind up in Greenville. En route, he must have passed hundreds of open and unlocked doors. It now was no comfort that the odds would have been long indeed that the last unlocked door he would ever enter was at the end of Third Street on a mill hill in South Carolina.

When Bounds, keeping his vow never to return to prison, died at his own hand in the kitchen of Mother's home, his father in Olympia, Washington, and his mother in Fedro Woolley, Washington, were notified.

Both refused to accept the body for burial.

The ordeal made Mother something of a reluctant celebrity for a time. Her attempt to pray for a killer, and to seek his salvation, became the subject of a number of sermons in the two Carolinas and Georgia in the months ahead. And she was asked again and again to relate what she went through that day two days before Christmas, and she always complied.

In the last three years of her life, Mother would regularly become a hospital patient. In 2001, she had to endure a long stay at St. Francis Hospital in Greenville.

When Doris arrived one Friday for her weekend hospital stay with Mother, she encountered one of Mother's nurses in the parking lot.

"How's Mother been doing?" she inquired.

"Oh, Doris, I hate to tell you this, but she didn't have a good night. She was hallucinating for a lot of the night," the nurse reported.

"What was she talking about?"

"It was awful," the nurse said. "For example, she told me that she and her granddaughter had been held hostage in her house by this man who already had killed two people that day. And that she and her granddaughter had survived, but the man killed himself."

Doris smiled. "Mother wasn't hallucinating," she informed the nurse. "That happened a little more than a year ago."

Mother and her granddaughter had physically survived the ordeal perhaps by befriending a stranger. But neither was ever again the same. In the silence of lonely nights, the ordeal would again and again haunt both women.

# Chapter Eleven

## *Golden Autumn*

Mother had entered the hospital in late summer when the land still was green but not many days before a golden autumn began to announce its arrival in the tips of the leaves on the maple tree just beyond the window in the room in which she was a patient.

Framed almost perfectly in that window, the middle-aged maple would become a reminder of the passing of time in the long days ahead, and of the hope that somehow once again Mother would join other senior citizens in climbing the three steps into the church van for the Young At Heart Club's annual trip to the mountains to view the colors of the season.

Spring, when the flowers came, and fall, when the trees were in their greatest glory, were Mother's favorite times of the year.

"When you get well, Martha," Granny Mitchell would remind her, "you and Nettie and I are going to the mountains again. Maybe all three of us will find a man this time."

Granny Mitchell always winked at one of us when she talked such foolishness.

Mother would always smile, and perhaps describe the sort of mountain man she preferred. It always sounded a lot like Dad, except the rich part. The running imaginary contest to see who would find a new suitor had been going on between Mother, Granny Mitchell and Nettie Brooks for years, certainly since a respectable stretch of time had passed since Dad had died. Granny Mitchell's husband, Carl, had died long ago as well, and too soon. Granny's husband once had been a textile league baseball pitcher of some note, but a strong case of fundamental religion had come his way and had convinced him that sports was the province of the devil. So, for the rest of his life, Carl disavowed any interest in further perfecting the art of throwing the curveball pitching instead the urgency of accepting God's salvation to anyone who would listen. And this he did with evangelical zeal. For Mother, Nettie and Granny Mitchell, it seemed better to talk of eligible men than to linger too long in their own lonesomeness. It was such a well-known subject of light conversation between the three widows that when more than 100 friends and relatives had gathered on a June day in the basement of their church to celebrate Mother's 90th birthday, a man dressed as a mountaineer came to lavish attention upon Mother. Granny Mitchell and Nettie, in on the prank if not the instigators, had pretended jealousy.

For Nettie, who used to phone Mother to tell her that she was sitting on her front porch of her home in the Glenwood Mill community watching men driving by, the birthday party skit had perhaps been something of a pay-back. Soon after Roger Childers became their new pastor, he was invited to be a guest at the Christmas dinner for the Sunday School class the three widows attended. The reverend's introduction to the group was not what he had expected.

"See that woman right there?" Mother said to the pastor, pointing to Nettie.

"Yes, m'am," he answered politely.

"Well, I want you to do something about her," Mother demanded.

"'Scuse me," responded the preacher, now clearly off stride.

"I said I need you to do something about her. Every time I get a man, she takes him away from me. Now, what you going to do about it?"

For a moment, there was silence. Granny Mitchell and Nettie, who were sharing a table with Mother, tried to pretend they had no idea what Mother was discussing with the preacher not far away. Finally, Preacher Childers found some diplomacy.

"Mrs. Browning," he said softly, almost apologetically, "I think I'd better just stay out of that."

Now, though, there would be little talk of finding the perfect man. As the days went by and Mother's condition remained troubling, the maple tree was keeping the cadence of the seasons. True to its own clock, the tree turned a mixture of greens and golds, then transformed into a blaze of color that Mother could only occasionally see as her body struggled to mend once again from some mysterious ailment that baffled even her doctors and surgeons. First, it had been her heart. Now this, this assailant they could not conclusively name. The recent months had not been kind, but Mother seldom complained.

Even when the maple began to lose its leaves and the golden autumn showed the first signs of turning to rust, there still came the words of hope.

"There's still a lot of color in the mountains," Granny would announce, stretching the truth. "You just get well and we'll go."

Now, Mother only smiled.

# Come Quittin' Time

I did my part in trying to inspire Mother some how to will her body whole again. Though I felt I shared with my sisters, Marlene and Doris, a foreboding that had been left mostly unspoken, I tried to hide it.

"You planning a big Thanksgiving?" Mother asked in mid-November on a day when she had heard that there was a telling chill in the air and for a time I was her only visitor.

"Same as usual," I answered, though at the moment I didn't know what "usual" was.

"I hope you have a great Thanksgiving," she said, her voice still strong.

"I expect I will," I responded. "You'll be home by then and we can all be thankful for that together."

She allowed silence to slip briefly back into the room, then reached to take my hand in hers before she spoke again, this time with a softness of voice I had not heard since my own childhood.

"Wilton," she said, calling me by my given name that long ago had been shortened by almost everyone except my wife and my mother and sisters, "this time, I won't be going home."

I tried to speak, to tell her she must be mistaken. Blocked by the growing lump in my throat, words would not come.

She still held my hand and looked into my face, and I into hers. There, in her countenance, was no fear, no dread; only a sense of peacefulness. Then she drifted off to sleep.

I sat alone, silently, in her hospital room. I looked out upon the maple which had lost most of its leaves now though a lone golden one, stirred by a frisky zephyr, waved frantically from the end of one branch that was now otherwise denuded of the golden cloak it had until only recently worn. The lonely leaf seemed frantic to join others of its kind being buffeted about by the same wind there on the ground. Was this a metaphor of Mother's life now? A woman of great spirituality, was she looking forward to what seemed now an imminent passage and to a promised reunion with Dad beyond that great river? I looked at my mother, now seemingly in deep sleep, her breathing coming regularly though softly. I brushed an annoying tear from my eye.

She doesn't *know* that she won't be going home, I silently argued with myself as I sat there. Such a thought that she would never again see the flowers she had planted and which she loved so much seemed somehow wrong. I could not imagine that house at the end of Third Street at Easley Mill without her, the house that had been the hearth for our family for more than 60 years. That house standing in the distance from that cotton mill where mother had spent so many hours helping create huge rolls of cloth of a quality that made her proud. Though I had been gone from that house except for visits for most of a half century, I could still hear the sounds of the house. The muffled scrapping and kneading as Mother spun her well-worn dough bowl in preparing homemade biscuits. Mother's cry of "Oooops!" as she hurried to rescue some bit of home cooking from her too-hot oven seemingly seconds before it burned, though we always found the results to be perfection. The sound of someone stepping on the metal grate over the floor furnace Dad had installed years ago just outside the door to the only bathroom, that bathroom with the door that always had stuck, though only slightly, so that it made a distinctive muffled thud when it was opened and closed. In my memory, I even could hear the closing of that door.

Mother turned slightly as she slept and hugged a pillow to the side of her face. Her slumber grew deep again, and I was left alone with my thoughts.

I knew Mother had been more fortunate than many. She had lived beyond her 90th birthday having never been forced by ill health or misfortune from the home she loved. Her own sister, Louise, had spent the last 10 years of her life in a nursing home, and I knew that Mother still felt pangs of guilt she did not deserve at having once found accommodations for her own mother in such a facility. Not surprisingly, her own choice always would have been to remain in that house on Third Street. And in that, she was most fortunate. Though Mother had first worked in the mill at the age of 12, before child labor laws were enacted, she had grown into her golden years unbowed by the back-breaking work. Until recently, her health had cooperated with her wishes and she still looked much younger than her age.

So, why take that away from her now, dear Lord, I wanted to ask. I sat there somewhat lost in my thoughts, not expecting an answer to my unspoken questioning of divine authority. "Why indeed?" I said, this time audibly though there was no one there to hear except for Mother who slept on.

"Why?" I repeated and for the first time now, I felt I understood a great truth:

This woman who had taught us so much about living and courage and faith, whose impact on our value systems was indelible and unmistakable, who never cheered our successes too loudly nor viewed our shortcomings too harshly, was teaching us one final lesson.

She was teaching us how to die.

In the days before Christmas, Nettie, fighting her own long battle against diabetes, was hospitalized and had a room a few doors down the hall from Mother's. Granny Mitchell still came regularly to visit the two of them, occasionally complaining good-naturedly about her own infirmities and pains, of which there apparently were many, especially since an automobile wreck had left her physically compromised. And Preacher Childers and Mother's Sunday School teacher, Wayne Capps, kept a vigil as did two of Mother's and Dad's close friends, Mamie and Odell Weaver. And there were others.

On the Christmas side of Thanksgiving, the first bright decorations of the approaching holiday season began to make their appearance in the halls and corridors of the hospital. A row of Christmas trees had been placed in a corridor off the main entrance and soon would be decorated to various themes by business and service organizations in our hometown. There would be a festiveness now about this place where Mother had come to die.

Then came a visitor we did not know. A Christmas visitor. Among Mother's many friends, his was not a familiar face. Walking with a slight limp, the frail visitor had come at the urging of his sister, who a day earlier had been one of Mother's visitors.

"I bet you don't know who I am," the man's sister had challenged Mother when she had arrived in the hospital room.

"Sure I do. You're Bessie Turner. You and I used to work together at Arial Mill," Mother responded despite the fact that she had not seen her old co-worker for close to 75 years.

The two old mill hands talked for a time, sharing memories, calling names from a distant past. Then it was time for the visitor to take her leave.

"My brother has been wanting to talk to you for years," Bessie said. "Do you mind if he stops by to see you in a few days?"

"Of course, I don't mind if he wants to come," Mother responded.

And now he had come and there was the obligatory small talk. "I hope you're doing well," he said.

"Pretty well for an old woman," Mother responded with a smile. And there were comments on the weather. Both Mother and the stranger knew this conversation was not what had drawn him to her bedside.

"I need to tell you something," he finally said.

"OK," Mother responded.

"I know you don't remember me," he said, pausing for confirmation.

"I know you're Bessie's brother," she answered.

"Yes, m'am," he said. "But you're somebody special to me. I've been wanting to talk to you for years and years and to say thank you."

"What did I do to deserve thanks?" Mother asked, now even more curious.

"It was 1935, maybe '36," he said. "I was five or six years old. And it was just before Christmas. You gave me some hard candy in a clean, white handkerchief that you tied with a pretty ribbon."

He smiled, and his old eyes grew watery.

"Did I?" Mother said softly, aware of the emotions of the stranger.

"Yes, m'am," he said, and his emotions now seemed strained with the memory. "It was the only thing I got for Christmas that year."

He paused, choking back more tears.

"And, Mrs. Browning, it was the best Christmas gift I ever got."

In the days ahead, Mother grew weaker seemingly by the hour and doctors I had never seen came from time to time to look in on the old mill hand, checking monitors, adjusting settings, and sometimes doing nothing. The days on which we could have a conversation with Mother became less frequent until mid-December. Much of the time now, her utterings were incoherent to us and precious were the moments when we could if only briefly tell her we loved her and be rewarded with a smile.

A few days less than two weeks before Christmas, I arrived to find her awake and when I stood at her bedside she looked up in obvious recognition. As she had done a few days before Thanksgiving, Mother reached and held my hand, this time in both of hers.

Her smile was angelic. Then she spoke.

"This is my beloved son, in whom I am well-pleased," she said. Startled, I understood the incredible significance of that from my Mother who faithfully read the Bible every day she could and whose beliefs were unshakable. How many times had she read those very words at the moment of Christ's passion? It took my breath away.

They were the last words Mother ever said to me. In those words, Mother had given me a Christmas gift of unimaginable richness. A Christmas to last me the rest of my days.

She soon lapsed into a coma from which she never again emerged.

When Mother died, Marlene walked down the hospital corridor to the room where Nettie was a patient.

"Nettie," Marlene said softly. She never got to deliver her message.

"I know, Marlene," Nettie said. "She's gone. I felt it when she died."

"Yeah, Nettie," Marlene said softly. "She's gone."

Sheltered as best we could against a biting wind and a cold, driving rain, we buried her beside Dad on Christmas Eve, and on the 68th anniversary of their marriage. In Mother's stilled hand was a white rose, placed there by Nettie.

An important part of the old mill hill had died. From that hillside cemetery, the old mill, now little more than a hollow shell, can be seen. It was there that Mother and Dad had worked and it was in that neighborhood that they had raised the three of us.

In her day, Mother was known as an expert at changing travelers, tiny C-shaped slivers of metal that were essential in guiding cotton thread onto bobbins in the spinning room. Mother's job had been to continually inspect the tiny appliances for the rapid wear for which they were known. Then using a standhook, a tool that looked like a misguided screwdriver with an angular notch near the end, she would press a knee against a brake mechanism stopping the spinning action of the bobbin in question while she replaced the tiny metal guide. Once removed, the used, worn out flecks of shiny metal seemed always to become embedded in the hardwood floors of the mill and in the soft soles of the shoes Mother wore as she labored through the years. It was said that Mother was the most skilled changer of travelers anyone had ever seen.

People such as our mother were the lifeblood of the textile industry. Now quitting time had come for the old mill and the old mill hand.

When Roger Childers preached Mother's funeral on Christmas Eve 2002, he chose the ordeal through which Mother and Dee had come almost exactly three years earlier as the enduring testament to Mother's faith.

"Wouldn't it be something," Rev. Childers said from the pulpit, "if one of the first people to greet Martha when she got to Heaven was the murderer who held her and her granddaughter hostage?"

Mother's faith had never needed verification, and that thought was without great comfort for us in our grief.

# Chapter Twelve

## *One Last Journey Home*

I started the engine and released the brake letting my car roll slowly down the small hill at the end of Third Street at Easley Mill, that gentle hill on which I had learned to skate, from which my home-made iron-wheel wagon once had gone thundering toward the flat part of our street occasionally awakening third shift workers as it did, where on a Christmas morning many years ago I once thought I had found marks in the red clay that must have been made by Santa's sleigh. There had been pressure on me to accept the theory that there truly was no Santa Claus, but I had resisted and felt I now had proof in those drag marks in the bare earth. I had wondered, given what I took as irrefutable evidence, who could doubt the existence of Santa? There was proof in those "sleigh" ruts, never mind that there was no evidence of the prancing and pawing of each little reindeer hoof.

And now, as the car rolled slowly down the hill, it had been a long time since Santa's existence had been an issue in my life and many of the memories and the faces of the old neighborhood came rushing back.

# Come Quittin' Time

With her children who all were a bit younger than I, Frances Smith had lived there just across the street at the top of the hill opposite where mother had lived for more than 60 years. When we first moved two doors to a newer four-room house at the end of the street from what became known as the Newsome home, the Youngs had lived there where the Smiths for many years had made their home. Childless, the Youngs were neat to a fault; their lawn always trimmed, the steps to their porch always freshly swept, and in the front yard was a small pond in which goldfish swam.

The small pond long ago disappeared, but I remember gazing into the shallow water on a bitterly cold winter's day and seeing spots of gold seemingly suspended there in the ice. Come the thaw, they moved through the water once again in their constant search for tiny morsels of food. How those goldfish survived their icy entrapment seemed a mystery to me. It still does.

And there, next door to our house and sharing the shade of a huge oak tree was where Ina and Alvoid Galloway and their children once lived. I have always known the exact age of their oldest, Beulah Jane, because we share a birth date though she is a year younger than I. In the late 1940s, a quarantine sign had been tacked to the door of their home warning us all away when Beulah Jane came down with diphtheria. Every night we were reminded to remember Beulah Jane in our prayers and a portion of mine always went something like this:

"God bless Mother and Dad and Marlene and Doris and all the birdies and animals. And make Beulah Jane well ..."

We really didn't know what diphtheria was. We knew more about polio which seemed rampant in what should have been our most carefree summers. We only knew that diphtheria was so much a threat to us all that the Health Department tacked the quarantine sign on the door of the Galloway house and we kept our distance. Beulah Jane survived, and so did we.

A mill hand by necessity and a shade tree mechanic by choice, Mr. Galloway, Beulah Jane's father, worked on the third shift at the mill. It was the graveyard shift which ran from 11 p.m. until 7 a.m., and he was known to fall asleep beneath the cars he was trying to repair. When he was awake he looked a lot like Roy Rogers to me and seemed always to have grease beneath his nails and lead in his foot. Still, I went along for the ride on one frightening trip to Greenville where he would purchase used auto parts. While rounding a curve near the city's old baseball field, Meadowbrook Park, I was certain that the old car came close to crashing. I always wondered if I would have been famous had I died that day because no one I knew ever died in a Hudson Terraplane and almost no one I knew had even taken a ride in one.

Mr. Hopkins, who had a problem with strong drink, lived there, in the house across the street from the Galloways and beside the Smiths. He once stopped me in the twilight of an early morning as I went door to door delivering the morning newspaper to inquire, with speech slurred apparently from a night of drinking, if I could tell him where he lived.

"Why, right there, Mr. Hopkins," I had answered, pointing to his house. "Don't you know where you live?"

"Sure, I do," he slurred. "I just wanted to make sure you knowed where I live."

I watched him climb the dozen or so steps to the front porch and then struggle to find the key that would open his door only to discover that the door, as usual, was not locked. Almost no one locked doors on the mill hill. "No need to," Mr. Hopkins had once said. "The only key I've got is a skeleton key and everybody else on the mill hill has a skeleton key just like it. So why bother?"

It was the Hopkins family who had a mixed breed dog, as were they all on the mill hill. It was a friendly pooch, gregarious and eager to run and play with neighborhood children and who always seemed to smile. Until the day an automobile ran over his hips paralyzing his back legs. In the weeks to come, he taught us much about courage; he learned somehow to lift his lifeless rear legs into the air and for the rest of his days, as best he could, he continued to follow us about using only his front legs. He seemed still to be smiling. For a lot of my adulthood, on those rare occasions when I have felt as if life might not be fair, I have taken courage in the memory of that wonderful little dog. I regret that his name no longer comes to mind because somebody ought to remember an animal such as that with so much courage.

And there, as the car rolled slowly along, was where the Newsomes - and before the Newsomes we Brownings - once had lived. They had a daughter named Opal who was older than I by several years. I once had a mild schoolboy crush on her, though neither she nor anyone else ever knew - until now. And the Garrens lived there, next door. I wondered if the pitting Jack and I left in the cement streetside curbs from hammering away to flatten the ends of axils for our iron-wheel wagons could still be seen. I didn't stop to find out.

Just across from the Garrens once were the Sizemores and their only child, a daughter named Becky who was a pal of my younger sister, Doris.

And the Dunns there, and the Whitlocks lived in the house at the corner. There the elder Mr. Whitlock could be seen on most pleasant days rocking peacefully on his front porch, watching the comings and goings along Third Street and Seventh Avenue.

Just across the intersection and the second house from the corner was the home of A.C. Walker who later left the mill hill and built his own home on South B Street. Mr. Walker was one of those perpetually friendly folk who once misunderstood what I had said when I knocked on his door to collect the weekly subscription of 35 cents for *The Greenville News* which I delivered.

"I'm here to collect for the paper," I had said when he had come to stand just on the other side of the screen door.

"You're here to do what?" he asked, grinning.

"Collect," I answered.

"Well, Wilton, go right ahead and clack," he said, laughing loudly. And for as long as I delivered his newspaper and came by on Fridays or Saturdays to claim the 35 cents he owed, the same greeting always was there: "Well, you're here to clack again." Early on, I decided that being more precise in my diction would now do no good.

But Mr. Walker was a generous man. His was one of the first telephones on our street and he graciously shared it with neighbors. My father once wrote to my uncle Jack, then a career Army non com, telling him about the Walker telephone. Jack promised to call the number from his far-away place of assignment on a particular day and at a specific hour. By prior arrangement, Dad walked down Third Street and sat with Mr. Walker on the front porch for a time until the phone rang and Jack was on the other end of the line. It was a wonderful thing, being able to talk to Jack so far away like that, Dad told us when he walked home once again. Mr. Walker did not charge for the service though he did accept donations to help pay the phone bill if one were so inclined. Dad gave Mr. Walker 10 cents for the privilege of talking with Jack, not bad considering that nearby, on the corner of Second Street and Seventh Avenue, men and boys lined up on the back porch on Saturdays for haircuts from Squalie Merck, who charged 25 cents per trim, same as the fulltime barbers up town. It was the same amount I charged for mowing a yard of grass with Dad's reel-type lawn mower.

Dad had been dead almost 13 years as I turned left onto Seventh Avenue, leaving my old street perhaps for the last time in my own life. And Mother, who was 90, had died when the Christmas lights were bright in 2002. And now the house, our home place if ever there was one, was being sold. The contract would be signed within days. Dad would have been surprised that the wonderful home had fetched something more than $65,000. He had rented it from the mill company when we were mere kids for 25 cents a room - a dollar a month. He then found a way to pay the unheard-of price of $3,500 for the dwelling in the early 1950s when the textile company decided to sell the houses on the mill hill. Dad doubted that, at that price, he would ever get it paid for, but he had, long ago.

Though a series of nine smaller houses had been built at the far ends of Second, Third and Fourth Street, and in various other vacant lots, perhaps some time in the 1920s, most of the houses on the mill hill had been constructed near the time the cotton mill itself was built with the industrialization of the South late in the 19th and early in the 20th centuries. The object was to lure young families from the farms and the mountains to the towns such as Easley through which rail lines had been laid after the Civil War. The mills, thus, could offer benefits that were difficult to turn down - well-constructed homes at 25 cents per room per month by the time Mother and Dad began their family. On other mill hills, for slightly more per month, the homes came sparsely furnished.

Though not every house in America yet had a garage with a new car parked inside, automotive transportation was not considered terribly essential. It was an easy walk to the job at the mill, company stores were placed strategically near the center of the community as were churches, in our case one for Baptists, one for Methodists and one for Wesleyan Methodists. The companies frequently even hired and paid the pastors who held forth Sundays and Wednesdays, and more often than that during revivals, in those churches. And therein lay a bit of mill hill elitism as well, though snobbery and mill hills seldom share the same sentences. When the church that would become important to us had been chartered in the early part of the century with my paternal grandmother as one of the founding members, the mill companies were pressured to exclude the fundamentalist Church of God congregation from the cluster of churches on the mill hill. "Holy rollers" we were called, and never in complimentary terms. The compromise became a promise from Alice Manufacturing Company, where most of the congregation lived and worked, of a building lot of the new church's choice in a then-undeveloped parcel of land fronting West Main Street on one end and the busy Atlanta and Charlotte Railroad Company - which became Southern Railway - rails of steel on the other.

The location became significant in getting folks to the altar. If the preacher timed his fire-and-brimstone sermon perfectly, the most frightening part would come just as a long freight train rumbled past in the distance and the whole building would tremble ever so slightly but enough so that the end of the world seemed closer than we had hoped.

The mill companies sought to minister not only to the souls of the hired hands, but to their bodies as well. Mills sponsored athletic teams, especially baseball, and the stars of those teams were lured to the neighborhoods by salaries that were believed to be slightly above the norm for other workers in the mills, and the athletes frequently drew better working assignments. In our neighborhood, they were often placed on "outside" crews which were charged with maintaining facilities including the homes. Then the homes were sold and about the same time textile league baseball became critically ill, finally mostly dying out in the early 1960s.

It had been a world in which many of us had grown up. If our parents dreamed of solid shift work in the mills as a way of escaping the farms and the backwoods life of their times, most of my generation dreamed of far-away places. Not many of us remained to become the generation of spinners and weavers who would watch an industry, weakened by foreign competition, wither on the vine and die.

# Come Quittin' Time

As I looked at the building in the distance that had once been *our* mill, it was easy to see the gaping hole in the walls at the south end where the heavy looms and frames and other machinery had been removed and apparently sold to keep other mills alive another day, or simply as weighty junk.

Everything had changed. Even scrub brush had found a home in the most unlikely of places, in the decaying mortar and brick at the very top of the mill's tall smokestack where coal smoke used to float aloft before any of us worried about pollutants and global warming.

I turned left onto Seventh Avenue. There, a short block away and on the corner was the house where the Browns used to live. Rodney, their son, was my age though larger than I. Like most mill houses, the Browns' had very little yard to front both Fourth Street and Seventh Avenue. Mill houses of the time had much more backyard than front, in theory, to give the people who had moved in off the farms a bit of land on which to grow vegetables, which most of them still did, and perhaps chickens. It was in those back yards where almost everyone on the mill hill planted Victory Gardens during World War II.

And like most of the kids who grew up on the mill hill, Rodney had a tough streak about him. For some reason he chose me as his daily punching bag and for weeks I tried to find new, different and safer routes home from West End Elementary in an effort to avoid Rodney. Too often, he still intercepted me, administered his beatings and allowed me on my way more bruised emotionally than physically.

Strange what thoughts come bursting forth in visits such as this. I slowed to a stop and looked at the front corner of that house. That's where it happened. That perhaps is where my life changed though I had not considered that until this very moment.

Weary of fighting and losing, I finally had decided that no matter Rodney's reaction, I would refuse to take anything but the most direct route home from school which passed just by that corner of the Brown house. I would walk down Fifth Street from the West End Elementary, turn left on Seventh Avenue just across from McCoy's Grocery, once a company store, right on Fourth there at the Brown's house, cut across on the path in front of the community house, where J.D. Searcy held weekly meetings as the community scoutmaster, then to Third Street and home. It therefore came as no surprise that when I rounded the corner at the Brown's house, walking more cautiously now, there was Rodney, waiting as usual, that scowl on his face once again, a beating with my name on it in the white knuckles of his balled-up fists.

"Been waitin' fer you," he snarled.

"Been waitin' fer you, too," I said, trying to sound far braver than I felt and surprised with the ease with which I said it. Suddenly, Rodney was there once again nose to nose and for the first time I landed the first punch hitting him squarely in the mouth. Rodney seemed shocked, but he also was hurt and he spat blood from his mouth. Suddenly, he was not as much concerned about me as about his own condition. He hurried up the steps and into his house and I walked on toward my home at the end of Third Street occasionally turning to see if anyone was gaining on me. No one was. I tried to whistle a tune and failed, but I was never a decent whistler even in less stressful times.

"How was your day?" Dad asked when I arrived home and dropped my books on the kitchen table.

"Fine," I answered, offering nothing more.

It would be less than an hour before my father would find out how fine indeed it had been. I listened out of sight in the room I shared with my sisters as Dad answered the knocking at the door. I recognized the voice of Rodney's father.

"Wilton hurt Rodney," Mr. Brown complained to my father.

"What did Wilton do?" Dad asked.

"Knocked two of Rodney's teeth out and I think you ought to pay for it."

"I don't think so, not after all the abuse Wilton has taken from Rodney since school started."

I was startled. How did Dad know that? Out of shame for not having better defended myself, I had never mentioned my daily encounters with Rodney, yet Dad somehow had known all along of my ordeal. In our lifetimes together, Dad would surprise me again and again in matters such as that.

The two fathers talked for perhaps another five minutes, each making his point on behalf of his first-born, and as far as I know Dad never paid Rodney's dental bill. I was proud that my father had stood up for me. I think Dad was smiling when later he told me, "Don't you hurt Rodney any more."

Now as I sat there, the car engine idling, I realized that the day Rodney and I met in battle for the last time was perhaps one of those very important days in my life. The incident now seemed filled with lifetime implications including a lesson on managing fear, particularly in career decisions. And that anticipation frequently is more unsettling than reality.

The more immediate result of my well-placed right haymaker, which I never saw since my eyes were closed when I threw it, was that it ended the last fight I ever had in growing up on the mill hill. Until then, my won-loss record in mill hill tussles was 0-for-life; I had never won a fight, though I had been an unwilling participant in many. But this time, word got around, spreading quickly among the neighbor kids that Rodney was missing two front teeth because of my lightning right fist, and no one ever challenged me again. For which I was thankful.

I pushed the accelerator once again, turned right on Fifth Street and drove along the street that goes past the old mill. For a moment I could look up the hill to Sixth Street and to the home in which Ralph (Coon) Hendrix had been raised and where, as far as I knew, he still lived. Years earlier, I had visited my old friend who had been one of the few members of my generation to remain on the mill hill and in the home where for years his parents, now both dead, had lived.

Ralph lived with his memories. The mill had been Ralph's life and when it died, so did a bit of Ralph's wonderful spirit. He had not found other work once the mill closed for good in 1991. Still, he remained the epitome of the generous spirit for which mill hill people are known. At some point in his early 60s, even Ralph's knees let him down and he was fitted with clanking braces to help maintain his mobility with, hopefully, a bit less pain. Still, Ralph cared for his neighbors, cutting the grass for people physically less fortunate than he. As we sat that day on the front porch of the house that looks down upon the mill below, Ralph had given in to his emotions. He had wept. He had lost so much, and now I too was about to lose my last link to my past save for my own memories.

Mother and Dad now were gone, and the house filled with so many memories soon would belong to someone I never knew. In less than two years, it would be for sale again at what seemed an inflated price. I fear that the old house, too, will soon show signs of yielding to the ravages of time, but I won't be there to mourn it. Still, someone ought to tell future owners how important that house really was. But so was every other house I now was passing. They all have history in their timbers, and ought to have historical markers out front. Every one of them.

To me, this mill hill always will be a special place even though the figurative footprints in the sands of our old neighborhood already were disappearing. I wondered how many of the people living on Third Street now know that once Willie Lee and Martha Browning lived and loved there, in that house. Or that Frances Smith lived there, and Aunt Nan there beside the home of Bess White, the Galloways next door to our house, that Mr. Hopkins always managed to make it the top of those stairs, and that the neighborhood had Garrens and Whitlocks and Sizemores and Walkers and Cothrans and Dunns and Sudduths and all the rest.

I pushed on the accelerator, modestly gained speed along Fifth Street and watched in my rear view mirror as the place of my youth disappeared from sight, perhaps for the last time.

# *Epilogue*

So, here we are, the three of us, free children of Southern cotton mill villages. With Dad gone now since 1990, and Mother since a few days before Christmas 2002, we are now the senior citizens in our families. I, in particular, have arrived at this point not certain what to do about that status in life. Aren't we supposed to understand so much of life by this time that we stand ready, even eager, to pass along nuggets of wisdom to another generation?

I don't know that I have great wisdom to pass along, but I think Mother would be surprised how much wiser, in at least one way, I have grown since she left us. By modern standards, neither of the three of us siblings gathered about us much wealth. But there were times, more than a few, in my life when I felt that Mother in particular had come to believe that I had more than I actually did. Perhaps more money, more leisure time and more options in my life. I thought she did not know about the long hours, the extra part-time jobs that once were necessary, the tight budgeting, or what it was like trying to stay awake on long drives through the night just to cover yet another in a lifetime of forgettable sports event.

"You've got a beautiful home," she said the first time she came to visit my family in the Western North Carolina mountains that for a time was home. "You ought to be very proud."

I thanked her for saying it. It, indeed, was a beautiful home, a beautiful place with a good view. And, yes, I was proud of it.

But it has taken me this long perhaps to understand what she must have meant in that and other comments, real or, on my part, perhaps imagined.

I also have said, and have written, that early in my life I determined that I would prefer not to earn my living in cotton mills as Mother and Dad had, and I meant it as no condemnation of the two of them as parents, and certainly as no disrespect. Still, I felt that my parents, and Mother in particular, saw that determination in me as an affront to all they had been. And the last time I wrote those words, in an earlier book, "Linthead," Mother's reaction was that I had badly misread her true feelings.

I wasn't convinced. I thought I was too insightful to have been very far off the mark.

My understanding is now different. My new perspective, unfortunately, comes too late for Mother's ears. But I now know that, for Mother and Dad, mill work was hard, the hours seemingly endless. It was honest work that provided subsistence for the day, but precious little for the future. It was OK by strictly profit-based textile standards to give one's life to the mill, but once that life was used up and labor no longer physically practical, the old mill hands were left to God and Social Security, and very little else to show for all the years of faithfulness to the loom. For Dad, and especially for Mother, the work started early in life and ground on for more than half a century. People don't work 50 years or more at anything any more, including commitments to lifetime partners. Now I know, in part because

I also have reviewed my hopes and dreams for my own children, that my parents wanted something far better for me, and for the three of us, than they had.

They both were child laborers, Mother only slightly more than Dad. Though Mother became a child laborer to escape a deplorable home environment, the use of little ones as fodder for industry was even at the time a national disgrace, and still is.

In doing research for this book, I came across a haunting collection of poems written mostly early in the 20th century and dealing with issues of child labor. They are memorable now a century later because of their sadness concerning the plight of children. Such as the poem, *The Factory Girl*, written in 1905 by Walter V. Holloway and reading, in part:

> *Why is it, I ask, that the birds are free*
> *To flit over vale and hill,*
> *While I a life-long slave must be*
> *In a noisy, squalid mill?*
> *Does God love the birds, and hate me so*
> *That He fills my life with work and woe?*
> *Or can it be that there is no God,*
> *Save the factory master's cruel rod?*

Yet, for me, a child of the mill but certainly no laborer, there is no sadness in having come from that culture. I have said and written that growing up on a mill hill in the South was the perfect place for a child. And that there was a part of me that wishes that my own children had been so blessed. I suppose I will be saying that until my own final day because, in my case, that certainly was true. I *enjoyed* my too few years of growing up on the mill hill.

Would I do it again? You bet. But only if you could promise that I once again would have the same parents.

# Come Quittin' Time

Here, in my own twilight, I find myself hoping that Mother and Dad enjoyed our childhoods as much as we did because, as far as I know, neither of the three of us ever fully appreciated until now what childhood must have been like for the two of them, what never having those carefree times of their own when they were 8, or 10, or 12, or teenagers really meant. In my youth, I was eager to grow up; I now can see that they would have chosen to hold on to their own innocent years a bit longer. But that choice was not theirs.

Did they miss "hanging out"? Did they ever wonder what it would have been like going to the prom? Doing term papers? Studying for college entrance exams? Spending a week at summer camp?

Sadly, I never asked. They knew of some of those things, but only vicariously.

In the three of us kids living our childhood lives, there must have been many reminders of what they had missed in young years that were filled with such work as to rob youth of its excitement. Yet, if there was even a moment of personal despair, a moment of self-pity in either of them, I never saw it. Still, I wonder.

On a perfect day, from our house at the end of Third Street at Easley Mill, the music comes rolling across the acres when the Easley High School marching band is rehearsing outdoors. Many years ago, I was a part of that ensemble. Since then, I myself have heard that distant sound of trumpets and drums and marveled at how clear, how close it seemed. And I remembered being there.

"I heard the band today," Mother used to say to me on those occasions. "It sounded so good."

Stupid me! I thought she was talking about favorable weather conditions that would make it easy for the sound to travel. But from what I know now of her own youth, was she saying something else entirely? Wasn't she saying, perhaps, that she had been swept away into her own world of imagination, and in the few moments she could linger there it had been wonderful? For a moment, at least, satisfying her own what-ifs? Could she have been wondering that had child labor not been her lot, as a young student in high school, would she too have played a clarinet, or percussion, and dressed on Friday nights in a fancy uniform?

How could she not have wondered?

Perhaps hearing the band playing in the distance had elicited a series of reactions from Mother. Marlene suggested that in commenting that she had heard, Mother was letting me know that she was proud of me and saddened as well that, as a second shift spinner, it was not possible for her to attend high school football games to hear close-up the sound of the band of which I was a part in its halftime performance.

There is something to this theory. When Marlene in her turn dressed in a long gown and took special care and attention to her appearance in other ways in getting ready for the prom or the nights the school chorus, of which she was a part, was performing, Mother always had special instructions for her. Once perfectly dressed, Marlene always had to go to the mill, in long gown climb the steps to the floor on which Mother worked, and apparently submit to Mother's approval.

We know now that Mother was not concerned that a button might go unfastened without her review, or that a zipper might stick. It was Mother's only chance to "participate," to be a part of what Marlene was about, to see her daughter dressed so beautifully even if the thunder of the machinery around her made it difficult for her to tell Marlene she was proud of her and loved her.

Mother knew what she was missing and stole glimpses of our youth in any way she could. We are the poorer for not having understood that a long time ago.

# Come Quittin' Time

When it came to her children, Mother truly was the "mother hen." When as a teenager, Doris announced rather boldly that she intended to spend a few days at the beach - "mixed bathing" was considered a mortal sin in our church - Mother reacted in an unexpected way.

"Well, come on," she told Doris. "We've got to go to town and buy you a bathing suit."

Robinson's, a clothing store on Main Street, was the favorite shop for most of us on the mill hill, as it was with the Brownings. But Mother was in a particularly proud mood and instead went marching with Doris into the shop of one of the clothiers who almost never catered to mill hill folk. Snooty sales people avoided the two of them; still mother chose one of the more expensive bathing suits for Doris, paid in cash, turned without a word and walked out triumphantly.

Child labor perhaps had stolen Mother's youth, but it put steel into her character and a passion in her soul. And she spent a lifetime trying to improve upon that.

Only recently have I learned, through Marlene, that even into her 80s, Mother still was using second grade dotted-line paper in an effort to yet improve the rudimentary handwriting skills with which she was left when she last was part of an organized elementary school class, perhaps at age 7.

Turns out, Mother never stopped learning, never stopped trying. When Dad died in August 1990, Mother had to learn how to do something most of us take for granted, writing a check. In all of her life, she had never written a check to anyone or for any amount. So, what's so great about writing a check? What if you had never done it? What else that we take for granted had she missed? She must have thought about all the what-ifs. But she did not dwell on them.

In a sense, Dad was more fortunate. He found a way to join me in my youth, by helping form a Boy Scout troop, sponsored by the Easley Church of God, and then serving as my scoutmaster. And therein lie some of my most precious memories. I remember camping out with my father and other members of the troop on a cold snowy winter's night at the Blue Ridge Boy Scout Council's Camp Old Indian. We hunkered down in lean-tos while Dad found enough dry wood for a fire and kept it burning through the night so that the heat reflected back into our makeshift shelters. On a frightfully cold night, we were as warm and cozy as if we were home in our own beds. When I became an ordeal candidate in the Order of the Arrow, Dad also became a part of that service organization of scouting.

I appreciated Dad's commitment at the time. I appreciate it even more now as the pieces of his life and mine are examined with the advantage of my own looking back. I have known a lot of friendly people in my life, but other than my wife, Dad was my best friend. I never told him because I didn't know that myself until very recently.

I once worked with a man about my age who, like me, had grown up on a mill hill, one in North Georgia. For a time we knew nothing of the similarities in our teenage years in that regard. When it became known, I wanted to talk about it, to understand if his mill hill had been very much like mine. Of course, it turns out, all mill hills were pretty much the same. Pretty much the same iron-wheeled wagons, homemade kites flown so high into the spring sky that they became mere specks, the same language. Especially the language. Only mill hill people know what it's like buying a hot dog with chili, mustard and onions at the "junk" and topping it off with a Dr. Pepper with salted peanuts poured into the drink. Or waiting for the "dope wagon." Mill hill people never took toilet breaks at work; instead they visited the "water house."

I love the language and the traditions of all that, even if long ago I decided I also like the special language of newspapering. In trying to compare notes with the new acquaintance from another mill hill, what I discovered is that not everyone who came from a mill hill childhood wants that fact generally known.

That was reaffirmed not long ago when I attended an autograph session featuring my first book, "Linthead." "I wouldn't have that book if you gave it to me," one browser said, pointing to a copy displayed on the table before me.

"Why is that?" I asked.

"Because that's what they called me," he said bitterly. "And it wasn't meant to be friendly."

My view was and still is just the opposite. I'm a Linthead, and downright proud of it, mostly because I'm proud to be my parents' son.

What you need to know is that certainly for me, for my sisters, and for thousands of people like us born in the 1930s and later, there's a pride that goes with our birthright as cotton mill kids. There were a lot of people who worked a lot of hard, hot hours and who never had the options of enjoying childhoods themselves. It was they who gave us those carefree summers of our young lives.

And there now are precious few of those heroes left to see how we handled the special gifts they gave us.

God bless them all.

# Wilt Browning

## ABOUT THE AUTHOR

*Come Quittin' Time* is the third cotton mill life book by Wilt Browning following *Linthead*, about what life was like in mill villages of the middle of the 20<sup>th</sup> century, and *The Rocks*, the story of a good mill baseball team that for a season competed less than successfully yet made history at the professional minor league level.

Browning, a retired newspaper reporter, columnist and editor, also is the author of a true crime book, *Deadly Goals*. As a journalist who spent most of his career covering sports, Browning worked for the *Topeka* (Kan.) *Daily Capital* and *State Journal, The Greenville* (SC) *News, Charlotte Observer, Atlanta Journal* and *Constitution, Greensboro (NC) News & Record* and the *Asheville Citizen-Times*. During a six-year period out of the newspaper business in the 1970s, Browning also served as public relations director for two National Football League teams, the Atlanta Falcons and the Baltimore Colts.

He is the winner of a number of journalism awards, including his five-time selection as North Carolina's Sports Writer of the Year. For a decade he has served on the board of the North Carolina Sports Hall of Fame including two years, 2007-08, as the Hall's president.

Browning and his wife Joyce, the parents of five children who now are adults, make their home in Kernersville, NC.

# Come Quittin' Time

To request more copies of following books by Wilt Browning, please use the order form below or contact the author through www.publisheralabaster.biz

Come Quittin' Time __$20.00
Linthead ————$16.95
The Rocks ————$19.95

Please send me _____ copy/copies of Come Quittin' Time
Please send me _____ copy/copies of Linthead
Please send me _____ copy/copies of The Rocks

I am enclosing $_____ (please add $2.50 for shipping/handling for the first book and .50 for each additional book.)

Book Total          $
Postage and handling $
Total Amount Due    $

Please mail this form with your check or money order
(no cash or C.O.D.'s) to
Wilt Browning
Alabaster Book Publishing
P.O. Box 401
Kernersville, NC 27285
www.publisheralabaster.biz

Name: _____

Shipping Address: _____

City: _____ State: _____

Zip Code: _____

167

Wilt Browning

CPSIA information can be obtained
at www.ICGtesting.com
Printed in the USA
FFOW04n0336151116
29402FF